THIRD EDITION

Growth and Welfare
in the American Past

A New Economic History

DOUGLASS C. NORTH
University of Washington

TERRY L. ANDERSON
Montana State University

PETER J. HILL
Montana State University

PRENTICE-HALL, INC., Englewood Cliffs, New Jersey 07632

Library of Congress Cataloging in Publication Data

NORTH, DOUGLASS CECIL.
    Growth and welfare in the American past.

    Bibliography: p.
    Includes index.
    1. United States—Economic conditions. I. Anderson,
Terry Lee, 1946-   . II. Hill, Peter Jensen.
III. Title.
HC103.N6 1983   330.973   82-16520
ISBN   0-13-366161-X

Printed in the United States of America

10 9 8 7 6 5 4 3 2 1

Editorial/production supervision and interior design by Paul Spencer
Cover design by Photo Plus Art
Manufacturing buyer: Ron Chapman

ISBN 0-13-366161-X

Prentice-Hall International, Inc., London
Prentice-Hall of Australia Pty. Limited, Sydney
Editora Prentice-Hall do Brasil, Ltda., Rio de Janeiro
Prentice-Hall Canada Inc., Toronto
Prentice-Hall of India Private Limited, New Delhi
Prentice-Hall of Japan, Inc., Tokyo
Prentice-Hall of Southeast Asia Pte. Ltd., Singapore
Whitehall Books Limited, Wellington, New Zealand

Contents

Preface

Since the publication of the second edition of this book in 1974, new economic history has continued to demonstrate its vitality. Theories have been modified, new data have been uncovered, and both have helped to provide answers to previously unanswered questions. In some cases they have contradicted our previous understanding of history. At the same time, economic historians have formulated many new questions and challenged accepted views. This new edition recognizes the dynamic nature of economic history and attempts to present, in light of the best and latest research, a nontechnical reappraisal of America's experience with economic growth.

Another obvious difference in this revision is the addition of two new authors. Though the three of us have not written together before, we have shared a common interest in the application of economics to historical questions. By combining our knowledge of specific fields with our common interest in institutions, we hoped to take advantage of gains from specialization and economies of scale. We believe this edition reflects these gains.

There are three major distinguishing features of this book. First, it presents a theoretical overview of the reasons for and consequences of economic growth. In this overview we concentrate on the incentive structure inherent in the institutional framework. Second, we have provided succinct presentations of the major issues and findings in new economic history while still offering enough historical background for the reader to understand and interpret economic growth. Third, we have made an effort to set, at least in part, the agenda for future research. Rather than simply reporting on current findings, we press some of the unanswered questions and develop new theoretical ideas.

We believe this edition continues to bring new economic history closer to the more traditional framework of the historian who has emphasized the political, legal, and social environment within which economic decisions were made. We still emphasize, however, the importance of economic theory as a unifying framework for understanding history.

In order to have a short, readable book, certain issues are treated rather briefly or omitted. For the reader desiring a more in-depth treatment of economic history, several more lengthy new economic history textbooks are now available.

The basic structure of this book remains the same as that of previous editions. The early chapters provide an overview of the issues and the economy's development. These are followed by chapters that describe a period or a specific subject in more detail. Major issues in economic history are woven throughout the book. Added to this edition are seven "Lessons from History." Believing that past events can help us understand the present, we have written short essays integrating economic theory and history with present problems. These lessons are presented between various chapters and are independent of chapter material.

We are indebted to all of the scholars who have done the research which has clarified our understanding of America's past. The reviewers certainly improved the organization of the book and made sure that we were not leaving out important findings and issues. For improving our writing style, we must thank Mary Ann Keddington. The Center for Political Economy and Natural Resources at Montana State University provided technical support and research assistance through grants from the Scaife Family Charitable Trust and the Samuel Roberts Noble Foundation, Inc. Finally, we thank our students who have asked the relevant questions and forced us to refine our thoughts.

Douglass C. North
Terry L. Anderson
Peter J. Hill

Abbreviations Used in Citations of Published Works

AER	*American Economic Review*
AHR	*American Historical Review*
EDCC	*Economic Development and Cultural Change*
EEH	*Explorations in Economic History*
EHR	*Economic History Review*
GPO	U.S. Government Printing Office
Hist. Statistics	U.S. Bureau of the Census, *Historical Statistics of the United States, Colonial Times to 1970*
JEH	*Journal of Economic History*
JPE	*Journal of Political Economy*
NBER	National Bureau of Economic Research
SEJ	*Southern Economic Journal*
U.S. Cong. JEC	U.S. Congress Joint Economic Committee

List of Figures

List of Tables

I

Theory, Statistics, and History

Economic history focuses on two main issues: the economic growth, stagnation, or decline of a society; and what happens to people in the course of such growth, stagnation, or decline. The latter issue is a consideration of the relative economic welfare of groups. If as a society grew richer everyone's income were to grow at the same rate, this would not be a vital question. But we know that as growth occurs, some groups fare better than others. Even in a prospering society, the income of some parts of the society may actually be dropping.

We want to be certain that our analysis takes into account all the benefits and costs of the events we examine; that is, were there side effects that were not properly measured in our calculations? For instance, in examining nineteenth-century growth and the concomitant industrialization, have we taken into account the harmful effects of pollution and unsanitary conditions that existed in new industrial cities? Environmental effects are not new, but they have frequently been neglected by economic historians.

As we look at the American experience, then, we are going to ask and attempt to explain what factors influenced (1) the rate of growth of the economy and (2) the well-being of various segments of society as the country grew.

DOES THE EXPLANATION
FIT THE FACTS?

In order to talk meaningfully about growth and welfare, it is necessary to use economic theory and statistics. It is impossible to analyze and explain the issues in economic history without developing initial hypotheses and testing them in the light of available evidence. The initial hypotheses come from the body of economic theory that has evolved over the past 200 years and is being continually tested and refined by empirical inquiry. Statistics provide the precise measurement and empirical evidence by which to test the theory. *The inquiry is limited only by the existence of appropriate theory and evidence.* Of course, the development of new theories or the discovery of new evidence permits us to extend our inquiry and to make sense of previously inexplicable events.

Explanation of welfare and growth issues comes from economic analysis, and these explanations are tested by determining the extent to which they provide a "best fit" to the available evidence. Sometimes these issues can be directly resolved by accurate and precise measurements. For example, it is commonly asserted that one of the causes of agrarian discontent in the last third of the nineteenth century was that farm prices fell more rapidly than the prices of other goods. The validity of this assertion can be supported by getting good price indices of agricultural and other commodities during this period, and, surprisingly, available data show that agricultural prices did *not* fall more rapidly than other prices. Another common assertion is that the Civil War accelerated the economic growth of the United States and made possible its industrialization. The effect of the Civil War can be examined critically by using data on the rate of American economic growth and on the growth of manufacturing output. These show that the economy grew most rapidly in the decades before and after the Civil War, but very slowly during the war. Manufacturing output was already growing very rapidly before the war, and by any standards we were already a great industrial nation. So, neither assertion can withstand examination in the light of readily available statistics.

A more common assertion that defies simple statistical testing, however, is that society or groups were better or worse off than they would have been had "circumstances" been different. In subsequent chapters, we shall examine the following statements:

1. British policy was vindictive and injurious to the colonial economy after 1763.
2. The railroad was indispensable for American economic growth.

3. Speculators and railroads (through land grants) monopolized the best western lands in the nineteenth century, slowed down the westward movement, adversely affected the growth of the economy, and favored the rich over the poor.
4. In the era of the robber barons, farmers and workers were exploited.

These statements are really incomplete. If we are to make any accurate appraisals of the issues and of the welfare implications, we must rephrase them to read:

1. British policies were restrictive and injurious to the colonial economy after 1763, compared with what would have taken place had the colonies been independent during these years; or more precisely, income of the Colonies under British rule after 1763 was less than it would have been had the colonists been free and independent.
2. Income in the United States would have been reduced by more than 10 percent had there been no railroads in 1890.
3. A different (but specified) land policy would have led to more rapid westward settlement in the nineteenth century, a higher rate of economic growth, and a more equal distribution of income.
4. In the absence of the monopolistic practices of the robber barons, farm income and real wages of manufacturing workers would have been significantly higher.

There are three essential ingredients in this sort of analysis. First, the hypothetical alternative must be reasonable. It would not make sense to hypothesize a world of free trade as the alternative against which to measure colonial income, since that was not likely in 1763–75. Second, to construct the hypothetical alternative we must use economic theory and analysis to understand how an economy operates and how it would have operated under different conditions. Third, good statistical data are necessary to measure what actual income was, compared with the income to be developed in the hypothetical alternative. We do not mean to suggest that this method resolves all problems in measuring the relative welfare of people in the past. We may disagree about what a reasonable alternative is. We may even argue about the quality of the economic analysis used in creating the alternative. But there is no way to avoid using the hypothetical alternative in economic history, since it is implicit in every statement involving cause. Nonetheless, there are numerous pitfalls in such analyses. In order to unequivocally answer the question posed by the hypothetical alternative, we may need a general equilibrium model that tells us not only how everything might have been, but also how the difference would have affected subsequent growth and welfare in the economy. This is simply beyond the capacity of economic theory, and all we can do is try to come as close to the ideal as theory and evidence will permit.[1]

The best evidence for testing our theories is statistical data that precisely define and measure the variables. The development of such data during the past twenty-five years has made possible a revolution in economic history, even though we are still a long way from having all the information we would like to have. It is unrealistic to expect that economic historians will ever have all the precise, quantitative information they need to test all theories (although diligent digging has yielded, and promises to yield, a much richer mine of it than was expected), and here the more imprecise and traditional evidence found in diaries, records, and other literary sources must be carefully examined. The important point is that such evidence is a poor substitute for precise measurement, and historians must be careful of the weight they assign to qualitative information.

An additional point should be stressed. What actually happened to people and what people thought happened are often not the same thing. For example, it may turn out that the American colonists fared rather well under English rule and, indeed, that they would not have done as well under alternative systems. But the colonists, acting on the view that they would be better off under a different set of circumstances, fought a revolution, became independent, and changed American history.[2] Their actions were predicated on the views, right or wrong, that they held at the time. Thus, throughout economic history, we are as interested in trying to understand what people *thought* was happening as we are in trying to arrive at an accurate assessment of what actually *did* happen.[3]

---

[1] There is nothing novel about the use of the hypothetical alternative. The welfare statements cited are all paraphrases of familiar statements made by historians, and historical writings are replete with similar assertions. The novelty is in turning such assertions into testable propositions, and this necessarily involves the methods described in the text. The concept of counterfactual propositions (hypothetical alternatives) was originally examined in economic history in a pathbreaking article by John R. Meyer and Alfred H. Conrad, "Economic Theory, Statistical Inference and Economic History," *JEH*, XVII (Dec., 1957). In the literature of philosophy of science, counterfactual propositions have been extensively examined. See Nelson Goodman, "The Problem of Counterfactual Conditions," *Journal of Philosophy*, XLIV (Feb., 1947), and R.B. Braithwaite, *Scientific Explanation* (New York: Harper, 1960), pp. 295–318.

[2] Whenever such cases arise, there are two possible explanatory hypotheses: (1) that people were misguided in their economic assessment, or (2) perhaps more plausibly, that they were primarily motivated by other than economic issues.

[3] Since traditional textbooks in history usually carry a full account of what people thought was happening to them, this subject has been slighted in this very brief study except where it necessarily emerges in specific welfare issues, as in Chapters XI and XII.

EXTENSIVE AND INTENSIVE GROWTH

This book will lay out theories of economic growth and examine those theories in the context of American history. The reason for the economic historian's concern with the overall growth of society should be apparent. Just how well off people can be within a society depends on how many of their wants can be satisfied. Going back 200 years or less, we discover that most people lived poorly by modern Western standards. Their societies simply did not produce very much. It was, therefore, impossible for more than a very small segment of the population to have its demands met—a condition that still characterizes a large part of the world. The importance of economic growth cannot be overemphasized, for it is this growth that determines how many material and nonmaterial demands can be satisfied. Economic growth defined in terms of productive capacity means that we can have more goods and services, more leisure time, and a cleaner environment. It is possible for even the poor to derive more from a relatively short period of sustained economic growth than from redistribution. The consequences of compounded real per capita growth at 1.6 percent per year dwarf all other welfare effects in our history. The prime issue to be understood, then, is how the Western world achieved growth that makes possible a standard of life undreamed of in past centuries.

The term *economic growth* has two distinct meanings. When people say that a city or a region grows, they usually mean that the number of people and the amount of business activity increase. There is an increase in output because more people, capital, and land are being put to productive use. This is sometimes called *extensive growth*, and it has always been a major part of America's development. In the eighteenth and nineteenth centuries, the territorial boundaries of the United States were filled out; foreign capital and millions of people came from foreign shores to help in the process. This extensive growth meant an increase in the output of goods and services, but it did not necessarily mean the growth of output per person. Economists see the latter as the crucial aspect of growth, since it is concerned with how well off individuals are on average. A society is materially better off only if it is capable of producing more output per person.[4] This is *intensive growth*, or the growth of individual, material well-being, and

---

[4] An important alternative is additional leisure. People choose more leisure in the form of a shorter workweek, and the decline in the workweek in the United States from approximately 70 hours to about 40 hours reflects a desire to substitute more leisure for additional output and income.

it can come about only if productive capacity grows at a more rapid rate than population.[5]

Before examining the sources of increasing per capita output (and its counterpart, the income people receive for producing that output, or income per capita), it is good to remember that scarcity is humanity's oldest problem. By necessity, it has always been the dominant feature of life on this planet. People have had to scratch out a living through much of the known past, and the degree to which they have climbed above subsistence has been limited indeed. Most of our history is a story of having just barely enough to survive. But the past two centuries have seen a dramatic change in the Western world, particularly in the United States, as society has soared above this level. Today, the problems of hunger, famine, and subsistence are not as major in America as they once were.

The per capita output of most of the world is still very low (see Table I.1). The figures in Table I.1 were arrived at by taking the total income of each country, dividing by its population, and then translating from that country's currency into equivalent dollars. Many limitations are inherent in making comparisons of this sort, but this method gives a rough approximation of comparative levels of living and illustrates that only a very small percentage of the world's population lives by a standard that most Americans would consider even barely comfortable. If a dividing line of $3,500 annually per person is set, more than 75 percent of the world's population lives below this level, and it is primarily the countries of the Western world that have exceeded it (Japan and the oil-rich nations of the Middle East are the main exceptions).

EXPLAINING ECONOMIC GROWTH

Why have the United States and a few other countries been so successful while the rest of the world has been so ineffectual in achieving a high standard of living? As with any other question in economic history, to answer this we must begin with an examination of the theory. The neoclassical approach to the performance of the economy presumes that individuals maximize utility or wealth and that this maximization is constrained by the availability of natural resources, human and physical capital, and technology. Let us examine these in more detail.

---

[5] This suggests the further complication of an increase in population in response to rising income. In many parts of the world there has been a Malthusian response to increasing total output, so output per person has not increased.

TABLE I.1   Per Capita GNP 1978 (in U.S. Dollars)

Low-Income Countries ($0–360): 53% of World Population

Kampuchea, Dem.	Viet Nam	Afganistan
Bangladesh	India	Central African Rep.
Lao PDR	Malawi	Madagascar
Bhutan	Rwanda	Haiti
Ethiopia	Sri Lanka	Mauritania
Mali	Guinea	Lesotho
Nepal	Sierra Leone	Uganda
Somalia	Zaire	Angola
Burundi	Niger	Sudan
Chad	China	Togo
Mozambique	Benin	Kenya
Burma	Pakistan	Senegal
Upper Volta	Tanzania	Indonesia

Middle-Income Countries ($361–3,500): 23% of World Population

Egypt	Ivory Coast	South Africa
Ghana	Nicaragua	Costa Rica
Yemen, PDR	Colombia	Brazil
Cameroon	Paraguay	Uruguay
Liberia	Ecuador	Iraq
Honduras	Dominican Rep.	Romania
Zambia	Guatemala	Argentina
Zimbabwe	Syrian Arab Rep.	Portugal
Thailand	Mongolia	Iran
Bolivia	Tunisia	Yugoslavia
Philippines	Jordan	Trinidad and Tobago
Yemen Arab Rep.	Malaysia	Venezuela
Congo, People's Rep.	Jamaica	Hong Kong
Nigeria	Lebanon	Greece
Papua New Guinea	Korea, Rep. of	Singapore
El Salvador	Turkey	Bulgaria
Morocco	Algeria	Hungary
Korea, Dem. Rep.	Mexico	Spain
Albania	Panama	Israel
Peru	Taiwan	
Cuba	Chile	

Industrialized Countries ($3,501–14,890): 24% of World Population

Poland	Libya	Canada
Ireland	Austria	Norway
USSR	Japan	Germany, Fed. Rep.
Italy	Saudi Arabia	United States
Czechoslovakia	Australia	Denmark
New Zealand	France	Sweden
United Kingdom	Netherlands	Switzerland
German Dem. Rep.	Belgium	Kuwait
Finland		

Source: The World Bank, *World Developmental Report, 1980* (New York: Oxford University Press, 1980), pp. 110–111.

Classical economists, most notably Thomas Malthus, believed that the limits of the natural resource base would constrain our ability to grow, since population pressure would increase demand at a rate faster than supply. To the extent that the resource base can be expanded, Malthusian population pressures can be avoided. Throughout most of American history, natural resources, especially land, have been abundant and have contributed to our growth. As we shall see, however, the contribution of the natural resource base to growth has not been large. When we combine this with the knowledge that many of the countries listed in Table I.1 have large resource bases but low per capita incomes, it appears that an explanation of growth based on natural resources is inadequate. Furthermore, some countries, such as Japan, have a very small resource base. Resources will constrain wealth, but they constitute neither a necessary nor a sufficient explanation for growth, the environmental and energy crises notwithstanding.

The second constraint on our productive capacity is the availability of capital. Investing in human beings, in research to discover new techniques, and in plant and equipment (material capital) requires savings, and savings represent foregone present consumption. Economic growth, therefore, requires that people be encouraged to forego present consumption and save part of their income. People and governments (at the state as well as at the federal level) invest in university research; firms invest in research; parents send their children to schools and colleges; individuals invest in their own training; and firms borrow money from banks (where individuals have deposited their savings) to expand plant and equipment. We take these characteristics of our world for granted. But we should not. They are integral parts of the growth process that have developed in our economy but are conspicuously absent in much of the world.

Highly complicated modern technology requires its users to possess vast amounts of education, or "investment in human capital." First must come engineers and scientists who will modify and adapt their training to the particular needs of different countries. Since each country has different resource endowments and different prices at which labor and capital work, what is an ideal technique for one country needs modification for another.[6] Second, this technology must be widely employed, requiring a labor force with sufficient education and training to make efficient use of complex machinery and techniques. Third, as

---

[6] For example, a machine is made in America in light of the fact that labor may cost $8.00 an hour; therefore, the machine is designed to economize on labor. Such a machine may not be the most efficient type in India, where labor costs are a small fraction of U.S. costs, but the machine is just as expensive as it is in the United States.

society becomes more complex (as in urban, industrial economies like that of the United States), an array of educated professionals is needed to carry out the demanding tasks of a highly interrelated society. Most underdeveloped areas simply do not have these prerequisites. Before they can make good use of modern technology, they must make substantial investments in education. Economists would say that there is complementarity between physical capital (that is, plant, equipment, machinery) and human capital, which is the sum of people's accumulated productive attributes, acquired not only through formal education but also from on-the-job training and apprenticeship programs, from maintaining good health, and from all the other ways by which people can make better use of their abilities.

The complementarity between human and physical capital already suggests that investment in material capital plays an important role in economic growth. Thus, just as investment in education and on-the-job training contributes to productive capacity, investment in plant, machinery, and equipment can also accelerate growth. Trained human beings together with material capital can efficiently exploit new techniques.

As with natural resources, the availability of capital has proved to be neither necessary nor sufficient for growth. When physical and human capital has been provided to lesser-developed countries, it has been left to depreciate and has produced little. If capital is to contribute to the productive capacity of a society, there must be proper incentives for individuals to forego present consumption and utilize the capital stock.

Technological progress has been the main response of economic historians to the question of successful growth in the Western world. The Industrial Revolution has been viewed as a kind of watershed in man's experience; on the far side of it man was doomed to live at low levels of income, while on the near side substantially higher standards of life have been attainable.

People of 200 years ago would be more at home 1000 or even 1500 years earlier than they would be today. In the past two centuries, life has been incalculably transformed by radical changes in technology: (1) the substitution of machines for manual labor (a change made famous by Adam Smith in *The Wealth of Nations*); (2) the development of new sources of energy, the most famous of which was the development of the steam engine during the Industrial Revolution, but more recently the internal combustion engine, the turbine and hydroelectric power, and nuclear power; and (3) the dramatic and revolutionary advances in transforming matter to make it useful for mankind, such as turning common coal into luxury textiles and fabrics.

A moment's reflection, however, should suggest that the technological source of growth alone is not a sufficient explanation of the unique American experience, since technical knowledge is available to everyone at small cost. Anyone who wants to use modern technology needs only to read scientific journals and to borrow from the research of the most advanced countries.[7] Therefore, if technological progress were the whole story of economic growth, all the countries in the world would be rich. As a matter of fact, some countries have not been able to make efficient use of technology; they have not been able to reach the potential that is evident in the Western world, particularly in America.

The study of economic growth from the perspective just noted teaches us that our theory is far from adequate. The basic reason for this inadequacy lies in the fact that neoclassical growth models assume an incentive structure that equates private and social rates of return. For the economic historian, this ignores interesting and important questions. The study of growth has taught us that institutions are important. Our task, therefore, is to integrate into the traditional explanation of growth an explanation of the kinds of property rights that formed the institutional structure and an explanation of why these property rights changed over time. Because this feature of growth is so important and because it underlies the amount of investment in natural resources, capital, and technology, it will be treated separately in Chapter II.

WELFARE: THE
DISTRIBUTION OF INCOME

Thus far in our discussion of the growth process, we have not mentioned the second major concern of economic history: welfare, or the distribution of income. How well did any group fare in its economic setting? In overall terms, the welfare of all groups is reflected in the distribution of income in the society, and changes in this distribution will mirror shifts in the relative well-being of different groups. Many of the major issues that confront the economic historian concern the real or alleged improvement or deterioration in the income position of a segment of society. The worker's standard of living during the Industrial Revolution, the discontent of the farmer in the late nineteenth century, and

---

[7] There is still no overall theory of technological change, although some interesting hypotheses have emerged in recent research. Note, however, that it is one problem to explain fundamental advances in technology and still another to explain the spread of existing technological knowledge.

the anti-poverty campaign in modern times are examples of such issues. Hence, another task of economic history is to provide the accurate quantitative data that is needed to measure the actual change in the income status of any group. Economic analysis is required to explain how and why relative material well-being changes and how these changes affect the institutional structure.

Though economic theory does not contain a complete explanation of how and why distribution has changed, the institutional approach of this book makes it clear that the answers to these questions are integrally related to the political system. An individual's share of income or wealth will be a function of the number of productive inputs owned by that individual and the value of those inputs. As we will see in Chapter II, the government has an important role in defining and enforcing property rights. Hence, through this role the government can greatly influence income distribution. In this book we intend to focus on how changes in property rights and the general institutional framework have affected the distribution of income and wealth. Since market forces will change the relative value of inputs, these forces will cause redistribution. In addition to these forces, and perhaps even as a result of them, the distribution of property rights also will change as the government defines and redefines ownership. The American Revolution, the Civil War, and the Great Depression are all examples of events in American economic history that were caused or at least influenced by the distribution of income. Since distributional issues have been at the forefront of economic history, this book will pay particular attention to the causes and effects of efforts to alter the distribution of income and wealth.

II

Institutions, Property Rights, and Economic Efficiency

The sources of sustained economic growth and the determinants of income distribution are to be found in the institutional structure of a society. Economic historians can no longer write good economic history without explicitly taking into account *in theoretical terms* the institutional structure of the system, both economic and political. We cannot avoid the political aspect, because decisions made outside the marketplace have had and will continue to have a fundamental influence on growth and welfare. Nor is it enough to use an *ad hoc* approach to politics, as historians have done in the past. Politics must have an integral part in the theory. We are a long way from putting together a comprehensive theory, but we can make a beginning.

INCENTIVES AND ECONOMIC GROWTH

While we stress that economic values are of major importance in making decisions, our analysis also recognizes the influence of noneconomic values. Wealth is whatever people think is responsible for making them better off. Under our definition, a view of a mountain, spending time with one's family, or a host of other nonmaterial activities are just as much a part of wealth as television sets and jewels. For example, when we examine the westward movement in the United States, we observe that people had a variety of reasons for their relocation: some were escaping from monotony, others from debt; some were seeking criminal activity, others were pursuing adventure; still others, like the Mormons, were hoping merely to be left alone. Yet, without denying the variety of motives that took people across the Atlantic or the continent, we can make economic sense out of their movements. More people moved when their destinations held the promise of potentially high rather than low economic returns.

For the economic system to work in the way we shall describe, it is not necessary for everyone to be motivated by economic gain. It is only necessary that a sufficient percentage of the population—often a small minority—be so motivated in order for a model of economic development based on the assumption of wealth-seeking behavior to provide fruitful hypotheses. Current economic analysis and economic history amply support this proposition, so we can turn to the critical element in economic development—the incentives provided by the institutional structure.

For growth to occur, the economic system must provide incentives for people to undertake productive activities; that is, it must encourage individuals to innovate, to invest in material and human capital, and to economize in general. Put more precisely, the private rate of return—the net return to the individual—should ideally equal the social rate of return, the net gain that society as a whole receives from a particular economic activity.

Two centuries ago Adam Smith described how individuals pursuing their own self-interest also improved the well-being of society. This is another way of saying that private and social rates of return do not greatly differ, although we should note in fairness to Adam Smith that he was concerned about just what kind of institutional structure would produce this result. But why should the two diverge? The answer is that sometimes property rights are incompletely specified or inconsistently enforced. In these cases there will be third-party effects, so that not all the gains and costs associated with an exchange are taken into account by the parties to the exchange. Defining and enforcing rights is sometimes so costly that it does not occur. Why? What are the implications of such a lack of definition and enforcement? Let us begin with several illustrations from American history and work back to the theory.

A major contributor to increased productivity in agriculture has been new production techniques and improved crop varieties. There has clearly been a positive social rate of return to investment in the development of this new technology. In fact, in some cases the social rate of return on investment in research has been as high as 700 percent (see Chapter VIII). With such rates of return, it is profitable for society to allocate capital to research and development. But the gains to society greatly exceed the gains to be captured by any private research organization. New varieties of plants or new production techniques are often available to all; it is difficult for the private firm to prevent its new knowledge from being used without charge. Hence, when there is a lack of clearly defined and enforced rights to ideas, we would expect a suboptimal level of resources devoted to agricultural research. The economic rationale for government policy designed to subsidize such research has been based on raising the private rate of return so that it is closer to the social rate.

Take a diametrically opposed example. In the last half of the nineteenth century, manufacturing cities grew up around iron and steel mills that were built near deposits of coal and iron ore in the Ohio Valley. The private rate of return was substantially higher than the social rate because there were significant social costs that the firms did not have to pay. The pollution of water and air was costly, but the costs were not borne by the steel mills; they were paid by the populace in terms of unpleasant surroundings, sickness, and mortality. Had these additional costs been taken into account (that is, if property rights in air and water had been accurately specified so that they could not be used without compensating those who surrendered their rights to such use), the rate of return to the mills might have been substantially lower. More important, it might then have been worthwhile for the steel mills to eliminate, or at least to work on eliminating, these undesirable side effects of production. The valuable resources used without compensation in this case were clean air and clean water. No private property rights in these resources were defined; but even if they had been, enforcing them would probably have been prohibitively expensive, given the enforcement technology of the day.

The cost of defining and enforcing property rights is often substantial. In the seventeenth and eighteenth centuries, ocean trade was beset by pirates and privateers who plundered ships and their goods. The enforcement of rights was frequently in the hands of the individual shipper, who had to incur the heavy costs of arming his ships and manning them with trained gunners. The costs to both the shipper and the ultimate buyer, therefore, were raised. One solution was to arm ships; another was to convoy them; a third, used by the British in the Mediterranean, was to bribe the pirates to leave British ships alone; and a fourth was to destroy the pirates, a method the young American Republic tried on one occasion against the Barbary pirates in the early 1800s. The choice of solution depended on the perceived relative costs and benefits of each. In this case, the problem was the enforcement of a well-defined property right.

PROPERTY RIGHTS AND EFFICIENCY

A market economy can be thought of as a vast web of complicated interdependencies brought about by specialization in the production process. In order for such a society to function well, it must have some social mechanism for communicating among the various parties, for coordinating individual activities, and for motivating individuals to undertake socially beneficial actions. A system of property rights that allows individuals to appropriate the benefits of the positive things they do for society, makes them liable for the costs that they impose on others, and allows for transferability of rights from one individual to another will generate this mechanism. The examples just cited reflect either the absence of well-defined property rights or the lack of enforcement, and they illustrate a breakdown in communication, coordination, or motivation. Markets pinpoint areas where people of diverse tastes, abilities, and resources can increase one another's welfare. The mutual gains available from voluntary production and trade create wealth and stimulate economic growth.

The capital formation and technological change discussed in Chapter I provide good examples of how communication, coordination, and motivation take place. If some individuals in society are willing to pay a premium for the use of other individuals' wealth, there is an incentive to save. Interest rates communicate the amount borrowers are willing to pay for these savings. Capital markets, particularly the banking system, coordinate and reward the borrowers and savers. The regional capital flows in the nineteenth century are a good illustration of this process.

Technological change in a market system also depends on well-defined, enforced, and transferable property rights. If an inventor or innovator received all the gains from the development and application of new knowledge (in other words, if the private and social rates of return were equal), then the incentives to develop new technology would be much greater than they are. But if an inventor spends years developing a superior machine only to see it pirated and used by others without compensation to him or her, then the inventor will receive only a small fraction of the social benefits, and the costs of years of research may well exceed these benefits. In order to encourage invention and innovation, we need institutional arrangements that will specify and enforce property rights in new ideas and their application to economic activity. One solution is patent laws, which attempt to give the inventor monopoly rights for a number of years; but even here the costs of enforcement make this a very imperfect solution. Eli Whitney found this out with the cotton gin, as he devoted years to litigation against those who appropriated his invention without compensation.

Likewise, the entrepreneur will act more diligently in the face of a well-specified rights structure. These activities will include seeking profit opportunities from new and cheaper ways of combining inputs, from providing services or products that others have previously not marketed, or from bringing together owners of and potential purchasers for resources. The entrepreneur must be able to purchase the inputs, to profit from sales of output, and to facilitate mutually profitable exchanges. Poorly defined rights (to either resources or income streams) will make it less likely that such entrepreneurial activity will occur.

THE ROLE OF GOVERNMENT

To understand how societies develop a property rights structure, we must understand government. Though the tools of economics have not allowed us to develop a comprehensive theory of the state, they do allow us a partial understanding of its role. We are not able to predict exactly when or how states evolve, but the use of economic theory has allowed us to specify more clearly the role of and constraints on government.

One of the basic reasons for the existence of the state is that it may be able to pursue some activities more efficiently than can other institutional arrangements. One such activity is the provision of protection and justice. Because the state has control of special coercive techniques or because of scale economies in protection and enforcement of property rights, a central body may be able to accomplish protection more cheaply. Since there are these potential gains from trade, members of society are willing to give up some of their resources to the state in the form of taxes and to grant government a legal monopoly on coercion. We shall refer to this as the protective role of the state.

In addition, the state may have a productive role since some goods, where exclusion of users is costly, will be underproduced in a market. In the case of these goods, the individual who cannot be excluded will tend to look for a free ride by not paying. To the extent that the producer of such a good cannot collect the full value of his production, a role for the state exists because its coercive power allows it to overcome the free-rider problem through taxation. For instance, a dam on a river that is subject to recurrent flooding offers substantial benefits to downstream farmers. Such farmers might view their gain from the dam as far exceeding their proportion of the costs. However, once the dam is in place, they cannot be excluded from benefiting from flood control. Therefore, it is to these farmers' advantage to not reveal their willingness to pay, in an effort to "free-ride" on the contributions of other farmers. In such a situation it is entirely possible that the dam will not be built, even though the benefits outweigh the costs. The farmers can solve this problem through government, by agreeing to coerce themselves—that is, to contribute through taxes in order that the free-rider problem can be avoided.

Thus, government can reduce uncertainty and generate order and stability, which in turn provide the climate for economic growth. Public goods, the production of which is difficult in a market setting, are made available, and an efficient set of property rights is defined and enforced, leading to a set of incentives that encourage growth. In this context the state exists because of a contract, implicit or explicit, between government and the people.

If all of the above is true, why is it that a government's role has not always been one of improving efficiency? To the contrary, the distinguishing feature of many if not most societies has been a set of rules or institutions that have not promoted efficiency or economic growth. Historically, attempts to constrain government to its protective and productive roles have not been very successful.

One basic reason why efficiency has not always prevailed is that it is by no means the only thing that improves individual well-being. Questions of equity or justice are also of crucial importance. In order for an efficient property rights structure to be chosen, it must be viewed as legitimate. The limitations on the size of the homestead under the Homestead Acts provide an example. Originally, only 160 acres could be taken by any one person. This was gradually expanded to 640 acres, but in many areas this was still less than the optimal size of an efficient unit. Despite a general awareness of the inefficiency of the Homestead Acts, equity considerations prevented land policy from allowing the unlimited purchase option. If a significant portion of the population does not think that efficient institutions are also fair, those institutions will be modified. Rules that do not have the moral sanction of the participants in the rule-making contract will be impossible to maintain.

Secondly, there is always the possibility that once the coercive power of government is established, individuals or groups will use that power for their own economic gain and in the process institute rights structures that do not promote efficiency. For example, throughout much of Western European history the crown found it to its advantage to choose institutions that created sharp divergences between social and private rates of return.[1] Likewise, individuals outside of government who desire to make themselves better off can pursue wealth and resource redistribution through that government. By investing time and resources in the process of influencing governmental decisions, the individual has the potential for earning an economic rent, a return in excess of opportunity costs. Hence, the coercive power of government, which is necessary for order, for the production of public goods, and for making the distribution of wealth more congruent with some generally accepted standard of justice, offers an opportunity for individuals to engage in what has been termed "rent seeking." Unfortunately, seeking rents through political favors requires that resources be expended to influence political decisions. Not only will these expenditures be made to gain rents, they will also be made in an effort to prevent wealth from being taken away. It is conceivable that the summation of resources on both sides could exceed the value of the wealth being redistributed. Since the resources consumed in rent seeking are not available for production, they represent waste (or deadweight losses) for society.

Thus the politicization of numerous decisions can seriously detract from the productive potential of the economy, particularly if large amounts of resources are used in rent seeking. This does not mean that government should never engage in the redefinition of rights or in redistributive activities; it simply means that we should be aware of the potential resource waste inherent in such activities.

Two examples help illustrate the problem. During the sixteenth and seventeenth centuries, France was definitely a rent-seeking society.[2] The crown had the absolute power to tax and regulate, and such power attracted many supplicants who were willing to expend resources to receive the favors they wanted. Most artisans succeeded in establishing guilds that regulated entry, conditions of apprenticeship, and hours of work permitted. Rules concerning manufacturing processes were so constructed that they provided effective limits on competition. The nobility and clergy were able to bend taxing power to

---

[1] Douglass C. North and Robert Paul Thomas, *The Rise of the Western World* (Cambridge: Cambridge University Press, 1973).

[2] Robert B. Ekelund, Jr., and Robert D. Tollison, "Mercantilism as a Rent-Seeking Society" (College Station: Texas A&M University Press, 1981).

promote their interests as well as those of their supporters. What suffered was the rate of economic growth.

A more current example is found in the tobacco price supports that increase the wealth of tobacco producers at the expense of taxpayers. The beneficiaries of such wealth will have an incentive to devote resources to convincing the government to affect transfers of wealth on their behalf. Potential losers in this process will have an incentive to resist such transfers. These activities reduce productive capacity by using resources in disputes over who owns what. In other words, arguments over ownership are costly, whether carried out on the battlefield or in the political arena. Not only are individuals discouraged from acting in ways that generate net social benefits, but the incentive structure gives them reason to use the state to gain control over resources. Furthermore, if the coercive power of the state can be used to take private property, the net private return from property will be less than the net social return, and efficiency will be discouraged.

An interesting question emerges from this discussion: What, if anything, prevents government from redistributing rights in ways that are compatible with neither efficiency nor equity? One consideration is the ease with which citizens can choose alternative governments. Just as competition in the marketplace limits the firm's ability to raise prices, competition among states will limit their ability to coerce. Historically, many states with a legal monopoly on coercion emerged because some individual or group had an absolute advantage in the use of violence. For example, the lord with his castle and knights was able to coerce his subjects since they had little ability to resist his power. In this case, the existence of scale economies and differential abilities in violence potential increased the coercive power of the state. On the other hand, in cases where there were few scale economies or few "trade secrets" in the generation of violence, there was less legal coercion. For example, in the mining camps of the American West, government's ability to coerce was reduced because the six-shooter evened out violence potential.

Two other constraints on government coercion emerge from the historical record. First, legal constraints in the form of constitutions have limited the scope and role of government. (In Chapter V we will emphasize the importance of this constraint in the United States.) Second, ideology has served to limit the coercive power of government. Though most economic models accept self-interest as the motivation for decisions, there is evidence that ideological considerations can restrain individual and governmental action. In the following chapters we focus on changes in these constraints, since they are crucial to the institutional climate in which the United States economy operates.

INSTITUTIONAL CHANGE

An explanation of changes in the rate of economic growth must include a theory of institutional change. We offer the following as the beginning of such a theory.

One result of an efficient set of property rights is that economic growth will occur. This growth is inherently destabilizing. Even though economic growth raises average per capita incomes, it can and will produce gainers and losers as wealth positions are altered. In some cases, the wealth changes are in absolute terms. For example, invention of the internal combustion engine significantly increased Henry Ford's wealth while it reduced the wealth of the many buggy makers. In other cases, the wealth changes are in relative terms. Investment in human capital, for example, will generally increase the wealth of the investor relative to that of the noneducated populace. Economic growth increases overall income, but the distribution of the increase is destabilizing. Changing absolute and relative wealth positions can create pressure for rule changes that protect the wealth status of potential losers, even if those changes lead to alterations in the incentive structures that produce inefficient results. Tariffs and subsidies that protect inefficient industries are good examples of this type of institutional change.

Also as a result of economic growth, there will be substantial changes in the organizational structure of society. One feature of technological change and specialization is alterations in the efficient means of production; more joint effort techniques are used. Work processes come to involve numerous individuals, and monitoring and measuring those individuals' contributions to output are difficult. Thus, large organizations arise, with ownership structures that depart considerably from tradition. These organizations significantly diversify the work experiences and the attitudes of the members of the economy.

Because of the changes just outlined, economic growth also affects people's ethical framework. The changing distribution of income brought about by growth produces changes in views about the legitimacy of certain wealth holdings. Specialization in the workplace leads to diversity of experience, which then produces different views of reality and different moral structures for organizing that reality. Historically, people lived in a setting with a high degree of moral consensus and community. Although there were many uncertainties related to one's chances of survival, there was no uncertainty about the basic moral framework under which people lived. Economic growth changed all of that. People moved to new jobs and new locations. Traditional occupations ceased to be profitable. New communication techniques

increased awareness about and perhaps dissatisfaction with position in life. There were fewer face-to-face encounters and less personalized exchange. All of this produced alterations in ideology, so that existing institutions were no longer as attractive as they had been. The bottom line is that efficient rights may well carry the seeds of their own destruction.

Before we conclude, one important caveat should be issued. This book does not argue that increased efficiency is good and income redistribution is bad. Indeed, we shall see that a majority of society may choose quite freely to give up some degree of efficiency in exchange for other values and may consciously vote (with varying degrees of success) to redistribute income from the rich to the poor.

A LESSON FROM HISTORY:

Do the Rich Get Richer and the Poor Get Poorer?

Economic growth always generates concerns about the unevenness of the rewards. Many believe that growth increases the incomes of those people at the top of the heap by extracting incomes from those at the bottom. Certainly economic growth has not affected all members of the economy equally, but do the rich get richer and the poor get poorer? What has been the distribution of gains from economic growth?

The answers to these questions, of course, depend on whether an absolute or relative living standard is used for comparison. When incomes of the poor are measured relative to those of the rich, the record in the United States has been uneven. During some periods of time the income distribution has become more unequal, while in others it is equalized. Recent work indicates that in the United States, income inequality widened from 1820 to 1860, stabilized until 1900, widened from then until World War I, and then lessened from 1929 until the present. The net result is an income distribution today very similar to the one existing in 1770.*

Even when inequality was widening, however, it does not follow that the poor were losing in an absolute sense. There is almost no evidence that economic growth actually decreases the living standard for people at the bottom, and there is much showing that their incomes were rising. Using income distribution figures and data on economic growth, the changes in real earnings of those at the bottom of the distribution ladder can be calculated. The results show that between 1770 and 1980, the bottom 20 percent of the income distribution increased their real income 7.7 times.† Other data corroborate this estimate. Real wages of the urban unskilled worker increased 4.5 times from 1820 to 1948.‡ Furthermore, the poor family in 1970 had a higher material standard of living than all but the richest in 1900.§ Therefore, while economic growth has not necessarily produced greater equality, it has provided the poor with greater access to goods and services by increasing their absolute incomes.

The debate over whether economic growth means that the rich get richer and the poor get poorer will undoubtedly continue. In the final analysis, however, a careful distinction must be made between absolute and relative measures of income.

---

* Jeffrey G. Williamson and Peter H. Lindert, *American Inequality, A Macroeconomic History* (New York: Academic Press, 1980).

† Calculated from Williamson and Lindert, *American Inequality, A Macroeconomic History* (New York: Academic Press, 1980), and Chapter IV, this book.

‡ Jeffrey G. Williamson, "American Prices and Urban Inequality since 1820," *Journal of Economic History*, XXXVI (June, 1976).

§ Stanley Lebergott, *The American Economy* (Princeton: Princeton University Press, 1976), p. 8.

III

The Development of the U.S. Economy: An Overview

Before examining specific issues of growth and welfare, it is useful to have an overview of the growth and structural changes that have occurred over the past three and one-half centuries. The topography of this economic landscape can be seen in the following tables and charts drawn from the accumulation of statistical data. They are supplemented at many points by the qualitative information gathered from the literature of economic history.

THE GROWTH RATE

The earliest national income estimate based on aggregate data is for 1840. Since then, per capita income has grown at a rate of about 1.6 percent per year in real terms (Figure III.1). That is, in terms of constant prices, the average per capita income has risen 1.6 percent yearly. This is roughly analogous to what has actually happened to the average standard of living or well-being of people, although we must remember that there are limitations to using per capita income figures in drawing too neat a pattern (see Chapter I). At first glance, 1.6 percent may not sound like a very impressive annual growth rate, but it turns out to have quite spectacular compound results. It means that every 43 years, income per capita in constant prices has doubled in America.

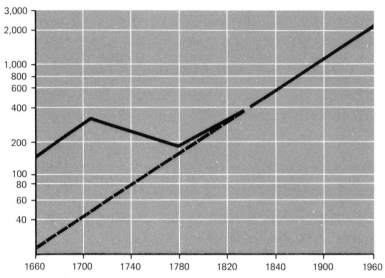

Source: Terry L. Anderson, "Economic Growth in Colonial New England: 'Statistical Renaissance,'" *JEH*, XXXIX (March, 1979), p. 246.

Figure III.1   GROWTH OF REAL PER CAPITA INCOME, 1660–1960 (1959 DOLLARS)

What happened before 1840? We lack information on aggregate income before that date, but we have known for some time that prior to 1840 per capita real income must have grown at a slower pace. Projecting the 1.6 percent per year growth rate back to 1680 indicates an income level far below what actually existed. Therefore, the rate of economic growth must have been slower at some time before 1840.

Though less is known about the economy, and the statistics are still far from adequate, historians and economists are piecing together evidence that clarifies our understanding of pre-1840 growth. It seems clear that from 1790 to 1840, real per capita income grew at about 1 percent per year. While slower than more modern growth, this rate is still rapid, enabling per capita incomes to double every 70 years. Data for the colonial period are even less refined. Furthermore, since growth prior to the Revolutionary War seems to have varied more by region, our understanding of aggregate growth remains tentative. It does seem likely that after the initial starving years, however, the seventeenth-century colonists did attain a rate of per capita expansion of between 1 and 1.6 percent per year. This suggests that the eighteenth-century colonial economy experienced stagnation and perhaps even decline (again, see Figure III.1). The evidence discussed in Chapter IV supports this inference.

THE COLONIAL ERA

What were the salient features of the colonial economy? First, 90 percent of the people farmed or worked in related pursuits. There were few technological changes in farming, but learning-by-doing did increase productivity and contribute to growth in per capita income. Some improvements in efficiency also occurred with increases in the size of the market and better marketing methods.

Meanwhile, substantial gains in productivity were taking place in another part of our economy—international shipping. In colonial times, America was already a major shipping power, engaged in fishing, whaling, and particularly in carrying the goods of the world—not only from our own shores to other nations, but also between foreign countries. Colonial productivity in shipping improved substantially during that period and became an important feature of the total economy. Much of the credit for the increased productivity goes to the reduction of turn-around time, but an event that we seldom think of today—the decline of piracy—also contributed. As the pirates were driven from the seas, fewer men and guns were needed for protection on ship. This saving was an important source for lowering the real cost of ocean transportation.

There was little manufacturing in the colonies. Shipbuilding was important, and there were some small-scale manufacturing activities like iron making; but by and large, it was a farming, shipping, and commercial society. Since America was a small market with relatively expensive labor, it is not surprising that the English provided most of our manufacturing.

It is clear that there was extensive growth during the colonial period. Rapid population growth characterized the era. Colonial population increased from negligible numbers to 331,000 by 1710, and then soared to more than 2,000,000 by the time of the Revolutionary War (see Figure III.2). Immigrants made up much of the increase, but by the eighteenth century natural reproduction was significant. Many immigrants came voluntarily, free and clear; but others put themselves into indenture, agreeing to work for a prescribed period of time in return for passage to America and for other specified benefits. During the eighteenth century, substantial numbers of people were brought in as slaves and provided much of the labor force in the southern colonies. Extensive growth during the colonial period, therefore, consisted of a notable increase in population accompanied by an increase in the labor force and an expansion of total output.

The colonial economy did not sustain growth equal to that of the post-1840 period, but there were regions that did approach this rate

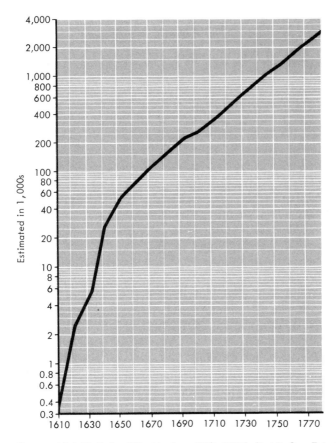

Source: *Hist. Statistics* (Washington: GPO, 1975), Part II, Ser. Z 1–19, T. 1168.

Figure III.2 POPULATION OF AMERICAN COLONIES, 1610–1780

for fifty-year periods. In the newly settled colonies such spurts of growth were sparked by the colonists' increased knowledge of the New World and by a growing demand for exports. The institutional setting that made private rates of return nearly equal to social rates of return provided the incentives for colonists to improve efficiency. Although growth during the entire colonial period was less than 1.6 percent per year, it was still substantial enough to allow a level of per capita income by the time of the Revolutionary War that was at least equal to Great Britain's and greater than that of most of today's world population.

This growth occurred despite the turbulence of the colonial period. The settlers frequently had grievances against the British, against the French and Spanish on their borders, against the Indians along the frontier, and against one another. At times, the conflicts led to open warfare. The actual income effects of these controversies have not been measured, but the most significant issues between the Crown and the colonists from 1763 to 1775 are examined in the following chapter.

THE NINETEENTH CENTURY

Beginning with the first census, in 1790, we can take a sweeping look at the economic pattern of the nineteenth century. Agriculture continued to play a predominant role in commodity output (see Table III.1). In 1839, when figures were first obtained, agriculture accounted for 70 percent of the value added. Certain agricultural commodities were particularly important. Of these, cotton played an early role and was a large part of total exports. In the years before the Civil War, cotton made up more than half of American exports (see Figure III.3). After the war, it continued as an important part of the agricultural economy, although the value of wheat exports began to challenge cotton's dominant position.

Agriculture expanded with the opening up and settlement of the West. It is not surprising, therefore, that as new, rich lands were developed, agricultural output expanded and agriculture diversified. Although agriculture grew throughout the century in absolute terms of value added, relatively it declined (see Table III.1). It was 70 percent of commodity output in 1839 and only 33 percent of output by the end of the century.

TABLE III.1   **Value Added by Industry in Current Prices, 1839–1899 (in Billions of Dollars)**

Year	Total	Agriculture	Mining	Manufacturing	Construction
1839	$ 1.04	$0.71	$0.01	$0.24	$0.08
1844	1.09	0.69	0.01	0.31	0.08
1849	1.40	0.83	0.02	0.45	0.11
1854	2.39	1.46	0.03	0.66	0.23
1859	2.57	1.50	0.03	0.82	0.23
1869	4.83	2.54	0.13	1.63	0.54
1874	5.40	2.53	0.15	2.07	0.65
1879	5.30	2.60	0.15	1.96	0.59
1884	7.09	2.84	0.20	3.05	1.01
1889	7.87	2.77	0.28	3.73	1.10
1894	7.83	2.64	0.29	3.60	1.30
1899	10.20	3.40	0.47	5.04	1.29

Source: Hist. Statistics (Washington: GPO, 1975) Part I, Ser. F 238–249, p. 239.

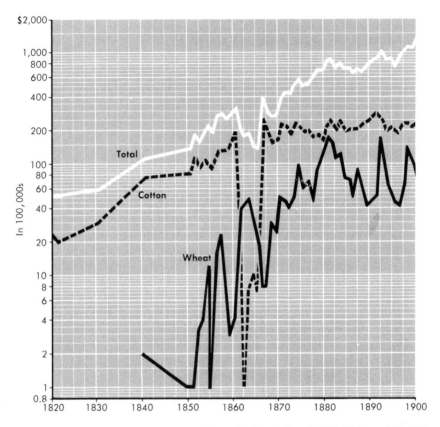

Source: *Hist. Statistics* (Washington: GPO, 1975), Part II, Ser. U 274–294, pp. 897–899.

Figure III.3 TOTAL EXPORTS AND WHEAT AND COTTON EXPORTS, 1820–1900

Labor statistics illustrate the same point (see Figure III.4). Out of 2.8 million people in 1839, 2 million worked on the land while other aspects of the economy were relatively negligible. As the nineteenth century progressed, however, there was a striking change in the employment pattern. It is true that the number of agricultural workers increased, but growing much more rapidly were the tallies of those working in manufacturing, construction, transportation, and trade. Later in the century, proportionately more people were working in activities other than agriculture. The peak year in absolute terms for agricultural workers was 1910, and the total has been declining ever since. The distribution of the labor force reveals that while we were a rapidly growing agricultural economy, other sectors—particularly manufacturing—were growing even faster. By 1880, only half of our people worked in agriculture.

When people shift from agriculture to other activities, we can expect comparable shifts in how they live. They will move off the farms to the cities, with the distribution continually moving in the direction of an increasingly urban society (see Figure III.5). By the twentieth century, America was becoming predominantly urban, but not until 1920 were there more people in urban than in rural areas. The westward movement and the shift from farm to city are tied to where people worked and the kinds of jobs they held. A sidelight to this pattern shows up in the birth rate in America (see Figure III.6). The decline

Figure III.4   AGRICULTURAL AND NONAGRICULTURAL LABOR FORCE, 1820–1980

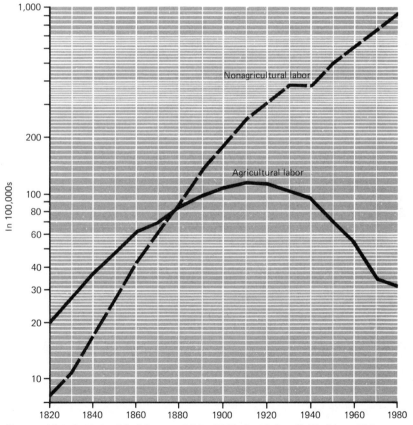

Source: *Hist. Statistics* (Washington: GPO, 1975), Part I, Ser. D 75–84, p. 134.

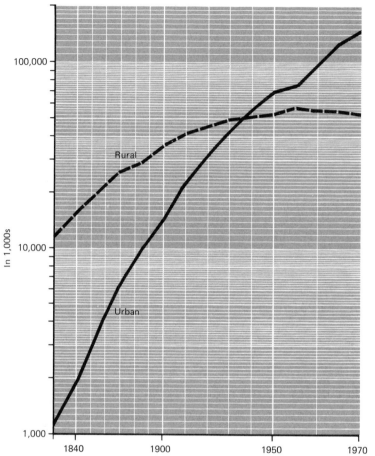

Source: *Hist. Statistics* (Washington: GPO, 1975), Part I, Ser. A 57–72, pp. 11–12.

Figure III.5   POPULATION IN URBAN AND RURAL TERRITORY, BY SIZE OF PLACE, 1830–1970

from 52 per thousand in 1820 to 22 per thousand in 1960 (and 18 per thousand in the 1970s) was first of all related to the shift from farm to cities. Children used to be much more of an asset on the farm and were less costly to raise than in the city. Today, farm birth rates are close to those for urban areas, generally confirming the fact that children are becoming relatively more costly in both city and country.

An integral part of nineteenth-century expansion was the growth of our banking system, of wholesale and retail marketing organization, and of a more efficient transportation network. All contributed significantly to increased productivity by lowering the real costs of credit and of handling and moving goods.

The high cost of carrying bulk goods in colonial times limited commercial production to areas adjacent to navigable waterways. Improved roads and turnpikes after the Revolutionary War widened local markets, but the major improvements in internal transportation came with the growth of water transportation on the Mississippi River system (particularly with the introduction of the steamboat in 1816) and the canal system that connected the Great Lakes with the Mississippi system and the eastern seaboard. After 1830, the railroad displaced the canal and dominated internal transportation (see Chapter IX).

The orientation of the colonies toward external markets and the purchase of goods from abroad led to rather well-developed merchant houses that dealt in exports and imports. But as internal trade and commerce grew, institutions to move goods from producers to consumers also grew, and they necessarily became more complex. The evolution from itinerant peddler, jobber, roving merchant, and general storekeeper (often associated with a local factory) to specialized wholesale houses and equally specialized retail outlets was a nineteenth-century development that was mirrored in the growing labor force engaged in trade, increasing from about 6 percent in 1850 to more than 10 percent by the turn of the century.

Banking was in its infancy in the decade after independence was realized. The first chartered bank was established in 1784, but the

Figure III.6   ANNUAL BIRTH RATE AND TREND, 1820–1960

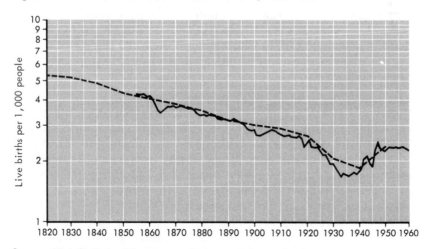

Source: *Hist. Statistics* (Washington: GPO, 1975), Part I, Ser. B 5–10, p. 49.

banking sector in general grew slowly in early years. The establish-ment of the first United States Bank in 1791 provided an important impetus for tying together government fiscal activities with the early banking community. Although the bank was an important step in the growth of the capital market, it engendered considerable opposition, and its charter was not renewed after its initial twenty-year term. In 1816, however, the second United States Bank was chartered. After a rocky start under undistinguished leadership, Nicholas Biddle estab-lished the Bank as a major influence in regulating commercial banks, in acting as a reserve bank, and in integrating the banking system. In short, it anticipated in many respects the role of a modern central bank in influencing the money supply and tying together federal gov-ernment fiscal activities with the banking system. The second Bank became an even more controversial institution than its predecessor and was a central issue in the presidential campaign of 1832. When Andrew Jackson triumphed, the Bank's fate was settled; and after the expiration of its charter, central banking was not to be revived until the next century.

The demise of the second Bank resulted in a mounting number of banks, each issuing its own notes. By 1860, there were 1,500 banks individually issuing an average of six different type of notes. The value of the notes varied strikingly: some were "as good as gold," and others were the worthless paper of broken banks. The Civil War and growing pressure for a national banking system led to the passage of the Na-tional Banking Act of 1864, which permitted the federal charter of banks and required that such banks keep reserves in cash or as deposits with a national bank in one of seventeen large cities. Similarly, banks in large cities had the option of keeping part of their reserves in New York City banks. A nationwide banking system was beginning. A cen-tral banking system to unite federal government fiscal policy with the banking system, however, did not occur until the Federal Reserve Sys-tem was created in 1914.

Also important to the economy, particularly in the first half of the nineteenth century, was our relationship with the rest of the world. We were but a small part of a large world, and the fact that foreigners wanted our goods and services contributed significantly to our expan-sion. Cotton and shipping have already been discussed, but foreigners also wanted other kinds of goods. Agricultural products in the early part of the century were in demand; and as the century wore on, other nations wanted our manufactured goods as well.

Perhaps more important than the role of trade in the country's growth was immigration (see Figure III.7). Beginning in the 1840s with the Irish famine and its consequences, vast numbers of people turned

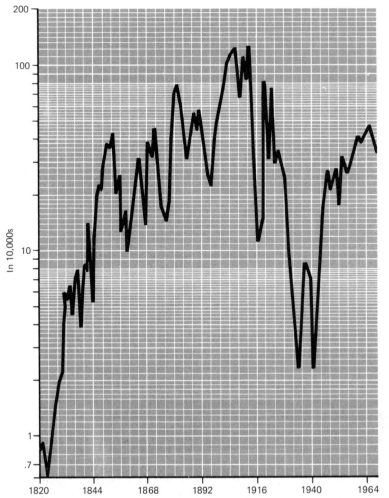

Source: *Hist. Statistics* (Washington: GPO, 1975), Part I, Ser. C 89–119, pp. 105–106.

Figure III.7   IMMIGRATION, 1820–1970

to America in a tide that continued until World War I. This was a swelling movement of unprecendented numbers willing to take their chances in a new world.

Foreigners invested heavily in the new nation (see Figure III.8). The British, having confidence in America's future, invested in canals, railroads, and cotton plantations. Although foreign investment was significant, it probably has been overtressed in the history of national

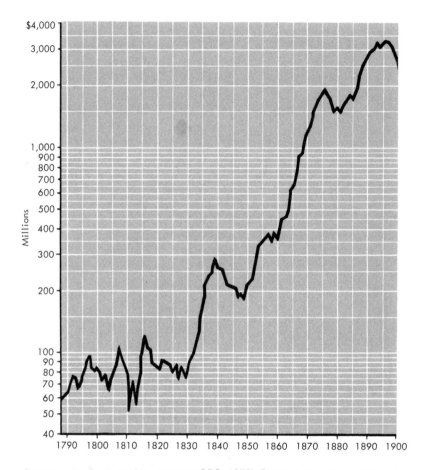

Source: *Hist. Statistics* (Washington: GPO, 1975), Part II, Ser. U 40, p. 869.

Figure III.8   FOREIGN INVESTMENT IN THE U.S. (NET LIABILITIES), 1789–1900

development. Foreign capital was important in the 1830s, but thereafter its proportion of total capital formation dwindled, even though the absolute amount grew substantially.

Overall, the international economy contributed through investment, through people, and through trade. We bought goods that could be produced less expensively elsewhere and sold goods that we could produce relatively inexpensively. It also contributed in an essential way that cannot be shown graphically—with ideas. The technology America borrowed in the nineteenth century, basically from Europe and particularly from Great Britain, was a major source of improvement in productivity.

By 1860, the United States was a major industrial nation, second only to Great Britain (see Figure III.9). America's progress into manufacturing predominance among industrial nations may be seen in Table III.2. From 23 percent in 1870, the nation's share rose to more than 40 percent of the world's manufacturing output by 1926–29. Between the Civil War and World War I, an already thriving manufacturing industry expanded enormously.

At the same time, population was being redistributed around the United States. By 1860, the populace was moving across the Appalachian Mountains into the Great Lakes area, into the Middle Atlantic area, and into the cotton-producing South. The Gold Rush of 1848 pushed the frontiers westward to California and Oregon. After the Civil War, movement was primarily across the Mississippi into the Plains, that vast area from the Mississippi to the Rocky Mountains. Population expanded from New England into the Midwest and then into the Far West (see Table III.3). Not only were people relocating, but they were moving into new and richer agricultural lands. As America rose to first

Figure III.9 COMMODITY OUTPUT IN FIVE-YEAR AVERAGES, 1839–1899

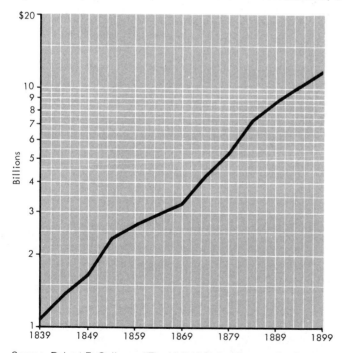

Source: Robert E. Gallman, "The United States Commodity Output, 1839–1899, *Trends in the American Economy in the Nineteenth Century*, A Report of the NBER (Princeton, N.J.: Princeton University, 1960), pp. 16 and 43.

TABLE III.2 U.S. Percentage of World Manufacturing Output (World = 100 percent)

Period	U.S.A.	United Kingdom	Germany	France	Russia	Others
1870	23.3	31.8	13.2	10.3	3.7	17.7
1881–1885	28.6	26.6	13.9	8.6	3.4	18.9
1896–1900	30.1	19.5	16.6	7.1	5.0	21.7
1906–1910	35.3	14.7	15.9	6.4	5.0	22.7
1913	35.8	14.0	15.7	6.4	5.5	22.6
1926–1929	42.2	9.4	11.6	6.6	4.3	25.9

Source: League of Nations, *Industrialization and Foreign Trade* (Geneva, 1945), p. 13.

place among manufacturing nations, it also became the world's leading agricultural nation.

The nineteenth century, therefore, was marked not only by an unprecedented increase in people, capital, and land, but also by an increase in productivity. First, America had adopted the most productive techniques in the world in manufacturing and in agriculture. Second, there was a significant increase in education, making possible the use of the latest technology and a new productivity stemming from research in industry and agriculture. Third, there was a new United States market of unprecedented size, which made feasible all the advantages of large-scale production.

Many efforts have been made to sort out how various factors contributed to the growth of the period. These efforts are fraught with theoretical and empirical problems, but they do give us some important insights. Table III.4 presents some estimates of those items that are responsible for increases in net national product. Of particular interest is how little the land supply contributed. It appears that resources were not nearly as crucial to economic growth as is usually supposed. Labor and capital are important contributors, and technological change or productivity looms large as an explanatory factor of our growth.

If overall growth characterized this period, so did frequently re-

TABLE III.3 Population Distribution by Region, 1870–1970 (in millions)

	1870	1890	1910	1930	1950	1970
Northeast	12.3	17.4	25.9	34.4	39.5	49.0
North Central	13.0	22.4	29.9	38.6	44.5	56.6
South	12.3	20.0	29.4	37.9	47.2	62.8
West	1.0	3.1	7.1	12.3	20.2	34.8

Source: *Hist. Statistics* (Washington: GPO, 1975), Part 1, Ser. 172–194, p. 22.

TABLE III.4 Percentage Contribution of Inputs and Productivity to Growth of Net National Product, 1840–1960

	1840–1960	1840–1900	1900–1960
Labor	42.7	47.2	34.8
Land	5.9	9.6	2.5
Capital	22.8	25.9	18.6
Productivity	28.6	17.3	44.1
Annual Growth Rate	3.56%	3.98%	3.12%

Source: Lance E. Davis, Richard A. Easterlin, William N. Parker, *et al.*, *American Economic Growth: An Economist's History of the United States* (New York: Harper and Row, Publishers, 1972), p. 39.

curring economic distress and hardship among diverse groups. The most important sources of such distress were the depressions and recessions of the nineteenth century. The years 1819, 1837, 1839, 1857, 1873, and 1893 marked the onset of falling income and increased unemployment of varying degrees of severity. Unfortunately, there are no accurate statistics to measure how much income declined or unemployment increased during these periods. But as a greater percentage of the population shifted from self-sufficient agriculture to production for the market, the impact of these depressions became greater as they affected more people.

As manufacturing grew, the immigrant or the farm boy who left home was likely to seek employment in the new factory towns. His hours were long and the conditions onerous. Factory towns were frequently unsanitary and overlaid with coal dust and housing conditions were grim. Although it is doubtful that the new factory worker's real income fell (see Chapter XII), he bore the serious costs of monotonous discipline during long hours at a machine and the possibility of unemployment as workers were let go during depressions.

The farmer's well-being, too, depended increasingly on the market. On top of drought, locusts, and other natural disasters, wide fluctuations in crop prices made his income subject to broad swings (see Chapter XI). The farmer's lot improved during the nineteenth century, but this overall improvement occurred while agriculture was declining relative to other sectors.

There were other changes in the economy that encouraged dissatisfaction. The dynamics of economic growth meant that all sorts of adjustments were required. The market signaled to various resource holders that it was necessary to shift to alternative employments. Agricultural production, for example, was moving West, where land was less scarce. Manufacturers that were resource dependent found that westward expansion increased their competition from firms that were closer to new discoveries of resources. Railroads were beginning to compete with water transportation, and shareholders in canal companies found their earnings decreasing. It should not be surprising, therefore, that the nineteenth century witnessed a variety of protest movements against working conditions, job insecurity, low prices, and monopoly.

Because of the changes in absolute and relative wealth, there was considerable pressure to alter the basic institutional structure of the economy. No longer did members of the society find the existing organizational framework desirable. Utopian schemes and programs of reform were continually advanced. Though trade union membership was never significant until well into the twentieth century, the founding of the American Federation of Labor in 1886 gave permanent national status to the labor movement. Farm protest movements had a larger impact on public policy. Between the Civil War and 1900, the Greenback, Granger, and Populist movements attempted to increase agricultural prices and to undertake basic economic reforms in the expectation that they would raise real farm income (see Chapter XI).

A source of mounting concern for workers and farmers was the development of the trust and other organizational forms with significant monopoly power. Henry Demarest Lloyd's *Wealth Against Commonwealth* and Ida Tarbell's *History of the Standard Oil Company* provided early examples of the proliferating literature of reformers and muckrakers who protested the growth of monopoly.

These dissatisfactions helped to produce a basic change in the property rights structure (see Chapter XIII). Beginning with *Munn v. Illinois* in 1877, the Supreme Court led the way with a series of path-breaking decisions that opened the door for rent seeking through government. The dynamics of growth in the nineteenth century produced pressures for change, culminating in constitutional interpretations that encouraged entrepreneurs to invest more in the political process to get special favors from government.

THE TWENTIETH CENTURY

World War I marked the end of an era, a boundary beyond which the world was considerably different. Nations were becoming more self-contained. America dammed the stream of immigration, and other countries erected tariff barriers. An international economy in which people, capital, and ideas had enjoyed free interchanges became hampered by restrictions on personal mobility and on trade.

World War I also marked the end of a relatively peaceful century and the beginning of century of global wars and depressions. The 1920s were prosperous, but the Crash in 1929 and the subsequent decade of depression resulted in a greater fall in income and a more cataclysmic economic period than any ever experienced before. The depression had long-run implications for how we would cope with comparable situations in the future and about the policies that would be pursued. The Depression continued in some measure until our entry into World War II in 1941.

In taking this overview of the twentieth century, a few salient changes should be recognized. One was the development of new products: the automobile, the electric refrigerator, and all other comforts known as durable consumer goods. There was also a vast demand for services relative to goods. Between 1919 and 1957, while nonagricultural employment doubled, employment in services tripled. As a result, there was a significant change in the employment pattern and in the economic structure to meet these new demands.

A second change was the turnabout in America's international role. Instead of being a debtor nation, as it was at the turn of the century, it became a creditor. Since World War II, the United States has spent vast amounts of money attempting to promote and assist the development of the rest of the world.

A third transformation took place in a change in the role of government in the American economy (see Table III.5). In 1790, the federal government spent only a tiny fraction of the national income and was involved in relatively few concerns. During the nineteenth century, taxes increased at less than 5 percent per year. Contrast this with the government's role in the economy today. Though federal employment

TABLE III.5 Compound Annual Rate of Growth in Federal Taxes and Employment, 1792–1970

	Taxes (Current Dollars)		Employment	
Period	Federal	Total	Federal Government	Total Government
1792–1974	6.40%	——	——	——
1792–1821	4.87	——	——	——
1821–1901	4.73	——	4.53%	——
1901–1974	9.54	8.08%	3.39	3.46%
1901–1929	7.12	7.29	3.21	3.43
1929–1951	13.70	9.59	6.88	3.40
1951–1974	6.81	7.58	0.74	3.56

Source: Allan H. Meltzer and Scott F. Richard, "Why Government Grows (and Grows) in a Democracy," *Public Interest* 52 (Summer, 1978), 112.

has not increased as rapidly as it did from 1821 to 1901, taxes have increased at a rate of more than 9 percent per year. Especially notable is the increase in both taxes and federal employment between 1929 and 1951. In 1980, the federal government alone (not state and local governments) had an annual budget of about $640 billion. Government at all levels spends more than one-third of total national income. Obviously, government today has a role different from any it has ever had before—one with more scope in regulating and ordering the working of the economy (see Chapter XV). This is clearly both a response to and the result of changes in the institutional framework of the society.

IV

European Expansion and Colonial Development

Colonial settlement was a direct outgrowth of the expansion of Western Europe in the fifteenth, sixteenth, and seventeenth centuries. The Western world was emerging from a relatively self-sufficient feudal society in which people produced most of their own goods, raised their own food, and made their own clothing and equipment. It was a world in which trade and commerce played a relatively minor role, a world characterized by the self-contained manor house and the small village it dominated. By the seventeenth century, the picture was changing.

THE EUROPEAN BACKGROUND

The conditions that had produced feudal society were: a lack of order, scarce labor, abundant land, and differential military endowments. In this context, serfs and free men provided labor services in return for the manor lord's protection and justice (embodied in the custom of the manor). In addition, the lord or state also produced some public goods. Population, which apparently declined because of the chaotic conditions that followed the collapse of the Roman Empire, began to grow again. But the lands around the manor could support only so many laborers before local returns to labor diminished. As a result, additional laborers had to work poorer land, and their output was less. Through-out Europe, however, there were vast lands still to be settled. We are used to thinking of the frontier movement as being associated with the nineteenth-century American West, but it is good to remember that *our* frontier was only a continuation of a movement that began—or to be more precise, was revived—as early as the tenth century.

As settlements spread throughout Western Europe, there were increased inducements for trade and specialization. The resource en-dowments of settled areas were diverse, with varying soils, climates, and topography. The cool, moist English climate produced excellent wool, for example, and the soil and climate of Bordeaux yielded fine wine grapes. Moreover, population centers provided an atmosphere for the development of different skills, and investment in human cap-ital varied from place to place. All of this added up to growing oppor-tunities for trade.

The growth in long-distance trade, together with increased pop-ulation, altered the conditions that had made the feudalistic system viable. Protection of production and transportation of goods and serv-ices were required in an exchange economy. Originally, artisans and merchants protected their own goods, but this protection could be un-dertaken more cheaply by a government that could overcome the free rider problem associated with public goods (see Chapter II). Further-more, as land became more scarce, its potential value increased; but as long as exclusive private ownership did not exist, no one could cap-ture those benefits. In England, the result was an evolution over cen-turies of private property rights in land.

The growing exchange economy, together with the increasing scarcity of land, therefore, led to a change in the state. The local manor lord typically provided protection and "law" in feudal society. The ex-change economy not only made local protection inefficient and useless for trade beyond the manor, it also altered the scale of warfare. In feudal times, a vassal provided knight's services to a superior lord for forty days a year. Given such limitations, large, permanent armies were impossible. Moreover, a distant army was no protection against marauding bands of Huns, Magyars, or Vikings. The local castle was the source of protection. But when vassals paid money to lords in lieu of knights' services, then lords could hire mercenaries, and the lord with the greatest resources could put the largest army in the field. New weapons also transformed the military. The longbow and the pike and then gunpowder, the cannon, and the musket made the heavily armored knight and the castle obsolete. All this required a large in-crease in fiscal revenues, and the only place to get the needed money was from the private sector. Princes competed to be able to provide protection or grant property rights in return for the revenues necessary to survive in an age of intrigue, conspiracy, shifting alliances, and expanded warfare.

There were two important consequences of this activity: First, the minimum size for survival of the state grew enormously, with the nation-state as the logical result. Second, the fiscal needs of princes were great, but since their bargaining power with their constituents varied from one nation to another and the structure of their economies differed, widely divergent patterns of property rights emerged with important implications for economic efficiency. In England and the Low Countries, kings were forced to give up much of their power to parliaments in return for revenues. The English Parliament gradually evolved and embedded into English common law a set of relatively efficient property rights. In Spain and France, absolutist monarchs emerged, and fiscal necessity immediately led to guild monopolies that discouraged innovation and the more efficient allocation of production factors. These developments are important, because as the frontier movement extended to the New World, the settlers carried with them the institutions of their homeland.

SETTLEMENT IN THE NEW WORLD

Following Prince Henry the Navigator's early explorations along the African coast in the fifteenth century, the Portuguese, Spanish, Dutch, and English explored, traded with, and settled new areas of the world, in some cases enslaving the indigenous populations. The Spanish and the Portuguese settled in South and Central America—the Portuguese on the east in what is now Brazil and the Spanish on the west up through Central America and as far north as Florida. The French settled Canada, traveled down around the Great Lakes, and followed the Mississippi River to what is now New Orelans. The British settled the coastal strip of North America from Maine almost to what is now the Florida border.

The American colonists emigrated for reasons as varied as their nationalities and their temperaments—for freedom of worship, for escape from political persecution, and also for purely business purposes. Obviously, the settlers who came were adventurous. The undertaking involved risks unthinkable to any but the most daring, and the colonists' courage was reflected in their social attitudes and in their determination to better themselves and to build a new life. The dissidents among them were continually struggling to improve not just the religious and political climates, but the economic climate as well. A main prerequisite to development—lacking today in some underdeveloped countries, but one that we inherited—is the combination of social attitudes that attuned America's colonists to economic growth. They responded quickly to economic incentives, thereby making the markets for labor and capital work better; and they tried to produce goods and services that were in demand elsewhere.

The institutions that the English settlers brought with them provided a hospitable background for growth. It is true that the Virginia Company and other early colonial ventures began by working land in common, but the disastrous consequences of this system quickly led to the *de facto* development of private property rights in land. The English joint stock companies also improved capital markets. Whenever investments in the New World brought relatively high rates of return, capital was quick to flow across the Atlantic. Finally, property rights in labor were well defined, even though in the case of slavery they were extremely unjust. Labor markets as we know them today existed in all areas of the colonies. In addition, the indentured servant system allowed migrants to borrow boat passage and provisions in return for labor services. While some have likened indentured servants to slaves, it is more appropriate to liken the system to a capital market wherein free men supplied labor services to pay for a loan. There is evidence that competition among creditors kept the terms of the indenture in check.[1]

These institutions prompted the colonists to produce goods that could be made most efficiently. The relative cost of each of these productive factors is determined by its relative scarcity or abundance. Abundance tends to lower price; scarcity elevates it. If many people demand capital to construct buildings, factories, equipment, and farms, then the price of capital will be high. Similarly, if a great deal of rich, productive land is available, the price of land will be low. This is the pattern that determined the form of production in the New World. Having abundant, rich land, scarce labor, and scarce capital, the colonies turned to agriculture, which provided the major source of economic activity for perhaps 90 percent of the population. If the concept of production according to comparative advantage were set alongside the natural endowments of the New World, it becomes evident why each region developed its own economic pattern. Each region's production possibilities were different. The incentive was to raise living standards by producing goods so efficiently that they would find a mar-

---

[1] David Galenson, "Immigration and the Colonial Labor System, An Analysis of the Length of Indenture," *EEH*, 14 (October, 1977), pp. 360–377.

ket outside the colonies and thereby make possible the import of other goods. The desire for efficient specialization divided the colonies into three major economic areas: the South, New England, and the Middle Colonies.

REGIONAL SPECIALIZATION

The South produced goods that fitted ideally the pattern that England had in mind for colonial settlement. It produced commodities that the English did not produce and that England and other countries wanted to obtain by trade. In the seventeenth century, the Chesapeake area produced large amounts of tobacco, and in the eighteenth century the lower South added rice and indigo to the export list. The difficulty with this pattern was that agricultural goods required not only an abundance of land, but an abundance of labor as well; and labor was relatively scarce and expensive. Indeed, in the colonial area, wages may have been as high as or even higher than they were in England. This led to efforts to import workers, especially for the southern plantations. Early plantation labor was supplied by free men or indentured servants. It was not until the late seventeenth and early eighteenth centuries that slavery became an economically viable alternative. When the price of indentured servants rose relative to that of slaves, southern colonists accepted slavery as a means of supplying labor to work on the plantations and to produce staple commodities such as tobacco to meet international demands. The pattern of trade and commerce in the South increasingly emphasized the export of such items, particularly to England and Europe, to finance the import of manufactured goods. In general, the value of exports to England exceeded the value of imports and thus conformed to Britain's mercantilistic hopes for colonial trade.

The situation in New England was totally different from that in the South. Although most people still earned their living from the soil, the land was relatively poor, except in a few rich river valleys like the Connecticut. Hence, a large number of people turned to other resources for employment. The sea provided fishing and whaling, and the land provided valuable furs and forest products that were essential to shipbuilding. As New Englanders became experts in fishing, their region became a major world shipping power, supplying ships not only for their own needs but for England's as well. The colonies shipped their own goods, such as fish, agricultural products, and wood products, to the Chesapeake and the West Indies. They also carried the goods of other colonies and other countries to the British empire and beyond.

As a result, shipping income became a most important factor in New England's economic well-being.

The Middle Colonies occupied the relatively fertile agricultural areas of New York, Pennsylvania, and New Jersey. In these areas, grain and livestock could be efficiently produced, and important seaports opened up access to the interior. This was a valuable combination, for the only efficient way to carry goods over long distances was by water. Rich land that lay far from navigable waters was handicapped

Figure IV.1   AMERICAN TOBACCO IMPORTED BY ENGLAND, 1620–1717

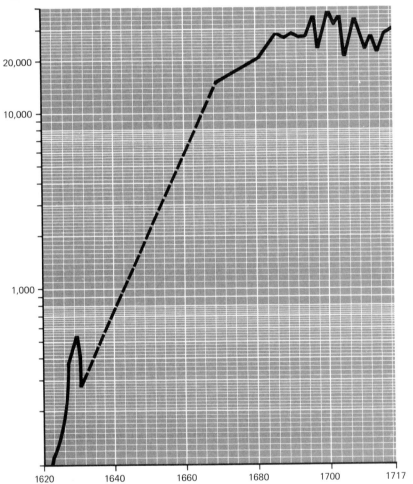

Source: *Hist. Statistics* (Washington: GPO, 1975), Part II, Ser. 449–456 and Ser. 457–459, pp. 1190–1191.

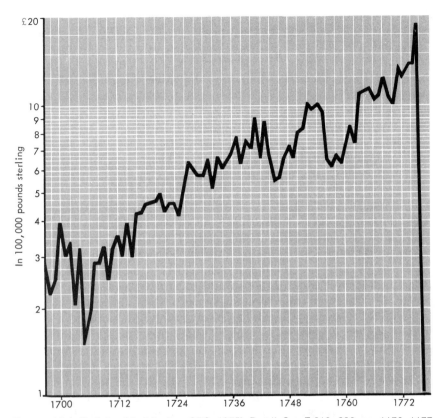

£20

10
9
8
7
6

5

4

3

2

1

In 100,000 pounds sterling

1700   1712   1724   1736   1748   1760   1772

Source: *Hist. Statistics* (Washington: GPO, 1975), Part II, Ser. Z 213–226, pp. 1176–1177

Figure IV.2   VALUE OF AMERICAN COLONIES' EXPORTS TO ENGLAND, 1697–1776

by the high costs of land transportation, and farmers on such land could offer their products for sale at a profit only if water transportation were available. As a result, New York and Philadelphia grew as collection centers of the interior's agricultural goods, and as shipping ports. Since the products of the Middle Colonies were by and large the things that the English themselves produced, the pattern of trade for the colonies came to be more with southern Europe and the West Indies than directly with England. In fact, the Middle Colonies imported more than they exported in their trade with England.

The pattern of development in the colonies is often referred to as *export-led growth*. The contribution of exports to colonial growth cannot be overemphasized. Immigration in response to high labor prices contributed heavily to population growth, but rising birth rates and declining death rates allowed natural population growth to dominate by the end of the seventeenth century. In turn, the larger labor force expanded the production of export producers. The 300-fold increase in the quantity of American tobacco imported into Great Britain from 1620 to 1717 (see Figure IV.1) is indicative of the export-led extensive growth during this period. The rise in the value of eighteenth-century colonial exports suggests that extensive growth continued until the Revolutionary War (see Figure IV.2).

COLONIAL PROSPERITY
AND INTENSIVE GROWTH

It has been clear for some time that the colonies experienced extensive growth, but only recently have economic historians uncovered the necessary data to measure intensive growth. If export-led growth were to yield per capita prosperity, gains from scale economies, specialization, learning-by-doing, or productivity change had to be made available to the producers. By and large, specialized agriculture, a vigorous export trade, and increasing shipping income made the colonies thrive.

Before examining the data on intensive growth, we want to reemphasize the importance of the institutional structure to colonial productivity. It is easy to take for granted the conditions that have encouraged people to become entrepreneurs in the marketplace. Gains from specialization and economies of scale clearly existed, but the important thing is that the colonists took advantage of these gains. The property rights structure in land, labor, and capital raised the private rate of return to the social rate of return and stimulated productivity. For example, the fact that property rights in land were well defined and transferable meant that, as settlements expanded, the optimal uses of any piece of land changed considerably over time. In the Chesapeake Bay area, land was first used for basic food production, but as the interior developed, the tide water areas came to specialize in commercial agriculture—in particular, the production of tobacco.

In Chapter III we discussed the general pattern of growth during the seventeenth and eighteenth centuries. Data for later periods tell us that sometime during the colonial era growth must have been lower than 1.5 percent per annum. Growing evidence suggests that this stagnation came during the eighteenth century, but there was substantial per capita growth in the seventeenth century. In the Chesapeake, for example, where tobacco production sparked economic activity, average labor productivity rose from 707 pounds of tobacco per year in 1619 to 2,351 pounds per year in 1699, suggesting productivity increase at the rate of 1.5 percent per year.[2] During the seventeenth century, marketing costs fell from 10 percent to 2.5 percent of the gross sales price, while standardized shipping containers cut freight rates in half.[3] The result of this productivity change was a 2 percent per year growth in real export earnings between 1659 and 1699.[4] Finally, wealth records for the period reveal a regional variation within the Chesapeake, but an overall trend that was at least 1 percent per year. The same kind of evidence for the eighteenth century suggests a stagnation of wealth accumulation at least until the middle of the century.

Prosperity in New England during the seventeenth and eighteenth centuries followed a similar pattern. Between 1650 and 1709 wealth and income per capita grew at a rate of approximately 1.5 percent per year.[5] Shipping, a major part of the New England economy, was experiencing substantial productivity increase (see Table IV.1). Both the manning of ships and the turn-around time in port were reduced dramatically. It does appear, however, that shipping was improving faster during the seventeenth than during the eighteenth century. Furthermore, data on wealth accumulation and agricultural productivity in eighteenth-century New England point toward stagnation and even decline.

Finally, the Middle Colonies, which were in their infancy in the 1600s, grew little during the ensuing 90 years. Agricultural productivity in this region dominated by agriculture rose 10 percent from 1714 to 1790,[6] with most of the increase coming during the first 50 years. This translates to a 0.2 percent per year growth in productivity, hardly comparable to the seventeenth-century experiences of the Chesapeake and New England. The overall picture of colonial growth is summarized in Figure III.1 of Chapter I.

In spite of the apparent decline in economic growth during the eighteenth century, there is little doubt that the average colonist was well off on the eve of the Revolution.[7] The mean income of the free

[2] Terry L. Anderson and Robert Paul Thomas, "Economic Growth in the Seventeenth-Century Chesapeake," *EEH*, 15 (October, 1978), p. 377.

[3] Edwin J. Perkins, *The Economy of Colonial America* (New York: Columbia University Press, 1980), pp. 51–52.

[4] Anderson and Thomas, "Economic Growth in the Seventeenth-Century Chesapeake," p. 377.

[5] Terry L. Anderson, "Wealth Estimates for the New England Colonies, 1650–1709," *EEH*, 12 (April, 1975), pp. 151–176.

[6] Gary M. Walton and James F. Shephard, *The Economic Rise of Early America* (New York: Cambridge University Press, 1979), p. 133.

[7] The following numbers were taken from Perkins, *The Economy of Colonial America*, Chapter VIII.

TABLE IV.1   Changes in Shipping Productivity by Commodity Route

Route	Commodity	Period	Annual rates of increase per annum (%)
New York–London	Bullion	1700–89	1.0
New York–Jamaica	Flour	1699–1768	0.8
Boston–London	Oil	1700–74	0.9
So. Europe–London	Wine	1650–1770	0.6
Virginia–London	Tobacco	1630–75	1.2
Maryland–London	Tobacco	1676–1776	0.7
Barbados–London	Sugar	1678–1717	0.9
Jamaica–London	Sugar	1678–1717	0.9

Source: James F. Sheperd and Gary M. Walton, *Shipping, Maritime Trade and the Economic Development of Colonial North America* (Cambridge, Mass.: Cambridge University Press, 1972), p. 69.

and nonfree colonist was $969 (all figures are in 1980 dollars), while the income of only the free colonist was $1,116 (see Table IV.2). The English mean income in 1774 was between $650 and $780. Thus incomes in the mother country were somewhat below those in the colonies. Comparing these incomes with the present (see Table I.1), we can see that the average colonist had an income greater than more than half of today's world population. In 1980, India had 15 percent of the world population and an average income of $400, while China had 20 percent of the world population and an average income of $700. The median colonial family in 1770 included five people with a total income of $4,225 ($845 per family member). The median U.S. Family in 1980 included 3.3 people with an income of $21,500 ($6,515 per person). From their infancy in the early 1600s, the colonies had attained a living standard that would have been envied by any in 1770 and even by a majority of today's population.

TABLE IV.2   Mean Wealth and Income by Colonial Region, 1774 (In 1980 $)

	Mean Wealth	Mean Income[a]
New England	$10,478	$702
South	$25,656	$1723
Middle	$12,298	$852
All Colonies	$16,380	$1116

[a] Mean income for free population only.

Source: Edwin J. Perkins, *The Economy of Colonial America* (New York: Columbia University Press, 1980), pp. 151–154.

BRITISH POLICY AND THE REVOLUTION

If the colonists were so successful under British rule, one cannot help but wonder why they fought so long and hard for independence. Discussion on this question began soon after the end of the Revolutionary War, and there is still no answer that satisfies all. Both economic and political factors must have entered into the decision. We will not try to put weights on these factors, but rather we will put British policy into an institutional context.

A deliberate policy of control over the colonial economy began in the 1650s, when the British imposed navigation laws designed to protect British shipping from that of the Dutch. The Dutch provided the most efficient shipping then available, increasingly carrying the world's goods; and shipping was too important as a source of world income for the British to let it go lightly. Part of their answer to the Dutch challenge was the promulgation of laws requiring that ships trading in the British Empire be built and largely manned by Britons or by British colonials. They further required that certain strategic or "enumerated" goods be shipped only to England. Tobacco was one of the goods from which the English merchants increasingly benefited. Since exports were so important to the colonies, it is not surprising that they complained about restrictions on their trade. Next, the laws demanded that European goods enroute to the colonies pass through England and English customs—another grievance for the import-loving colonists. The colonists were also prohibited from exporting certain manufactured goods, such as hats and wrought iron. Finally, to assure Britain's independent supply of certain important commodities, a bounty was declared on such colonial products as indigo dye and naval stores (pitch, turpentine, tar, and masts) that were used in all kinds of naval and merchant marine activities.

After 1763, when the British had concluded their costly Seven Years War and their exchequer was depleted, they felt that the colonists should shoulder an additional tax burden. As a result, Parliament passed several acts with names that are now grade-school history— the Stamp Act, the Townshend Act, the Sugar Act, the Tea Act—all designed to increase taxes on the colonists. At the same time, to prevent warfare with Indian tribes and keep defense costs down, measures were passed to keep the colonists from crossing the Appalachian Mountains.

Earlier, we saw how nation-states emerged from feudal society and undertook the protection and enforcement of property rights. The amount of taxes the state could collect depended on its bargaining

TABLE IV.3   Index of Per-capita Tax Burdens in 1765 (Great Britain = 100)

Great Britain	100
Ireland	26
Massachusetts	4
Connecticut	2
New York	3
Pennsylvania	4
Maryland	4
Virginia	2

Source: James F. Shepherd and Gary M. Walton, *The Economic Rise of Early America* (New York: Cambridge University Press, 1979), p. 163.

strength *vis-à-vis* its constituents. If the gains to the constituents were small and there were active competitors providing these services (the protection and enforcement of property rights), then the state could either collect minimal taxes or face revolt or a switch of allegiance. If, on the other hand, the gains to constituents were large—perhaps because all property rights were endangered by the threat of outside invasion or internal disorder or because the state had no close competitors—then it could demand much higher taxes. Thus the power of England to tax the colonies depended on the benefits offered and the costs imposed.

Assessing the costs and benefits to the colonists of being subject to British rule is not easy. For products such as tobacco there is no doubt that the return to the colonial producers would have been higher had the colonies been independent and able to export directly to continental markets. British trade policy reduced colonial well-being. The colonists also would have enjoyed somewhat better terms if they had been able to trade directly with the Continent (indeed, this shows up in the Confederation period as a lowering of import prices). On the other hand, independence likely would have reduced shipping incomes, since colonial shippers would have found themselves excluded from the West Indies trade and limited in their trade with other parts of the British Empire. New economic history has tried to systematically measure these benefits and costs. The result has been an endless controversy over the methods for measurement. But all studies agree with Robert Thomas's conclusion that the net burden was "not large."[8] Furthermore, data snow that per capita taxes in the colonies were a small fraction of those in the mother country (see Table IV.3).

[8] "A Quantitative Approach to the Study of the Effects of British Imperial Policy Upon Colonial Welfare: Some Preliminary Findings," *JEH*, XXV, No. 4 (December, 1965).

How does this explain the Revolution? First, the overall burden of being in the Empire was "not large"; but as the Revolution approached, a significant burden might have shifted to new groups who happened to be politically articulate and influential. The New England merchants, for example, suffered large additional costs because of the various taxing acts and retaliatory measures imposed by the British, such as closing the port of Boston.

But the point that deserves special emphasis in our institutional analysis is that British policy prior to the Revolution opened the door to further increases in taxes. Remember that the colonists came from a tradition wherein fundamental rules were important for limiting the role of government. The apparent stagnation of the eighteenth century is not inconsistent with the hypothesis that property rights were becoming less secure. To the colonists, the Quebec Act, the Stamp Act, the Tea Act, and other regulations were a violation of the implict constitutional contract with the mother country. The colonists had before them historical experience, where the Crown's control over taxes had gradually been wrested from it by Parliament so that arbitrary changes in tax rates could not be made without its consent. The revolt, however, was not just a protest against taxation without representation, but also a concern over government without limits.

A LESSON FROM HISTORY:

Did Indentured Servitude Improve Human Capital Markets?

Any student attending college is aware of the imperfections in the human capital market. Our banking system basically facilitates investments in physical capital, and these investments have contributed significantly to the economic growth of the United States. During the 1970s, however, economists began to realize the importance of human capital to the growth process. Unfortunately, financial institutions (the capital market) are not equipped to meet the investment in this form of capital.

A loan for the construction of a factory will include a mortgage on the physical property, but legal constraints preclude a similar mortgage on human services. The student attending college can expect a higher income as the result of his or her education. A lending institution, however, cannot legally require that a student loan be backed with a portion of future earnings. Therefore the risk to the creditor is higher on loans for investments in human capital.

Such an impediment to the human capital market has not always existed. During colonial times, individuals in the Old World signed contracts with agents who were responsible for clothing and feeding them and for providing passage to the colonies. In return, the indentured servant was required to work a specific number of years. In this way people with a few physical assets could borrow on their human capital to take advantage of the "land of opportunity." Contract terms were very specific and varied considerably depending upon the servant's age, sex, literacy, professional skills, and choice of destination. From his survey of 2,049 indenture contracts of British servants who emigrated to the colonies between 1718 and 1759, David Galenson concludes that

> a high proportion of the servants in the sample studied entered indenture contracts voluntarily, within the context of competitive market for indentures. The results indicate that merchants adjusted the term of service in view of the price the servant was expected to bring in the colonies. If coercion had played a large role in the recruiting process, merchants would have had no need to give more valuable servants shorter terms; that they did so indicates that they lacked the ability to force all servants into uniformly long terms. One reason for this inability was almost certainly the competition among the agents for recruits.*

Indentured servitude during the colonial period provided a human capital market that does not exist today. Migrants were able to move from the Old World to the New World with the expectation of earning higher incomes. Agents provided the necessary financing for this move and could secure their loans through the indentured contract. Today, legal constraints on capital markets prevent this kind of guarantee, thereby constraining human capital investment.

---

* Galenson, David, "Immigration and the Colonial Capital Market: An Analysis of the Length of Indenture," *Explorations in Economic History*, 14 (October, 1977), p. 373.

Suggested Readings:

Galenson, David, "The Market Evaluation of Human Capital: The Case of Indentured Servitude," *Journal of Political Economy*, 89 (June, 1981).

Heaver, Robert O., "Indentured Servitude: The Philadelphia Market, 1771–1773," *Journal of Economic History*, XXXVIII (September, 1978).

V

Years of Decision, 1783–93

The period from 1783 to 1793 was a time of decision for the new American society. Politically, during this period the form of a new government was chosen and a constitution was established. For the economy, it was a time to develop the basic rules of the game. In order to understand why the colonists chose the rules they did, it is useful to examine some of the major influences on their thinking.

POLITICAL AND ECONOMIC THEORY

In addition to their institutional inheritance discussed in Chapter IV, the colonists had important intellectual underpinnings for their views on rights and the role of government. A major tenet of colonial political philosophy was that government needed to be limited. The idea of limiting the powers of government goes back to the Magna Carta in 1215, but two men were crucially important in developing and articulating the concept of limiting the power of the state. Sir Edward Coke (1552–1634), chief justice of the king's bench, was the main proponent of the idea that common law, or the accumulated legal traditions of the society, was a check on arbitrary royal or popular prerogatives. This heritage came to be a significant part of England's unwritten constitution.

John Locke (1632–1704), another Englishman, was the second spokesman for limited government. Locke developed a more theoretical basis for limitations on government. His natural-rights doctrine argued that society does not create rights, but that an individual possesses these rights even in the absence of organized society, and that individual property rights follow from natural rights. On the basis of these rights, individuals could contract with others to form a civil society. His contract theory of the state argues that government is created by and dependent on the will of the individual members and has no separate power or rights of its own. It can enforce rights, but this power is legitimate only so long as the members (the governed) agree to be a part of the contract. It follows rather directly that if the social compact is violated, its members have the right to revolt.

The colonists were profoundly influenced by Locke's thinking, and when England violated what they felt to be their natural rights, they found it appropriate to revolt. However, their desire to limit government and to return to the institutional structure of the past gave the Revolution a strangely conservative color. Unlike most other modern revolutions, the American revolution did not promise utopia, nor did it find a need to remake all of society's institutions. All state and local governments were left intact, and contracts entered into prior to the Revolution were honored.

The Declaration of Independence well illustrates the colonists' belief in the contract theory of the state, the adherence to natural rights, and the responsibility of revolution when government violates the terms of the agreement. One of the interesting aspects of the document is the long and carefully drawn list of usurpations by George III of powers not delegated to him by the contract. Clearly, the colonists did not believe that "might makes right." In order to justify the Revolution, a careful statement of how the Crown had violated rights of colonists was made.

When the war with England ended, America faced all the problems that confront any new nation. To survive, it was necessary to create a viable economy. A government must be established not only to institute the political process but to make countless decisions, not the least of which are economic in nature. What should be the government's role in the economy? What responsibility should it have? How should a legal structure be developed to delineate the rights and the restrictions of private property? Where were tax revenues to come from, and how much should be collected? Where should the money be spent? To speak of taxes is to pose a double question: Who is to pay them, and who is to benefit from them?

Adam Smith published the *Wealth of Nations* in 1776, and with an insightful combination of historical observation, analysis, and polemic he described the workings of a particular set of institutions that would lead to the "wealth of nations." Smith is often portrayed as simply a proponent of *laissez faire*, or the idea that if left alone the economy will naturally gravitate toward an equilibrium wherein everyone is as well off as possible. This is an unfortunate misreading. Smith saw the invisible hand working to promote the social good only when private and social rates of return were equal. In fact, the *Wealth of Nations* was a study of the conditions under which self-interested individuals promote the good of society and under what circumstances such a pursuit is counterproductive. Smith described the framework for an efficient set of rights that would lead to a productive society.

Mercantilism, a system in which the government was involved in the economy in a variety of ways, was what the *Wealth of Nations* was attacking. Among other mercantilistic devices, bounties were paid to encourage the production of specified commodities, and monopolistic privileges were awarded to some companies, giving exclusive trading rights in particular areas. The aim was for the government and the economy jointly to promote national expansion and welfare at the expense of other countries.

Smith's diametrically opposed view was that mercantilism was an inefficient system that fostered monopoly and gave privileges to particular groups in the society. He found it to be the antithesis of how a society should be organized to provide maximum wealth for all people. To Smith, mercantilism was the very quintessence of the rent-seeking society.

In his works, Smith argued that the basis for economic growth was specialization and division of labor. Efficiency stemmed from employing enough people to produce a commodity so that their tasks could be specialized and, therefore, more rapidly and efficiently completed, since each person could concentrate on doing just one thing. In addition, if this specialized task were reduced to its narrowest possible form, then machines might be developed to do the work. In short, technological change would be encouraged by specialization. Since division of labor depends on the feasibility of producing on a large enough scale, the size of the market is a basic influence on specialization. A small producer, turning out just a few items a day, a week, or a year, will probably do all the work alone; but if the market increases, a larger number of workers will be needed. Each task can be specialized, and the producer can then institute a division of labor.

In a market economy, the one who organizes economic activity is the entrepreneur. The entrepreneur decides what will be produced, basing that decision on the relative returns from different kinds of pursuits. If it appears that making shoes will have a higher return than making bricks or hats, then shoes will be produced. But to start making shoes, one needs a location, equipment, and labor. Accordingly, one may borrow the necessary capital to buy machines, to build a factory, and to advance payment to the workers while they are producing the goods. While the entrepreneur decides what will be produced, being guided by relative profitability, the capital market plays a crucial role in financing the beginnings of production.

Adam Smith clearly understood that this type of productive activity could occur only within the correct institutional setting. The *Wealth of Nations* abounds with examples of situations in which the incentive structure was such that productivity was not encouraged. For instance, education is likely to be of poor quality, and professors will not care about the quality of their lectures if rewards are not based on performance. Smith also criticized the Crown's ownership of land, because such ownership did not provide the incentive structure afforded by private property.

THE ISSUES OF THE 1780s

With these ideas, Americans emerged from the Revolutionary War facing staggering problems. The new nation was deeply in debt to the French, who had helped with finances, munitions, and equipment, and to the American citizens who had loaned money to the Continental Congress. The problem was how, if at all, to pay these debts. A second problem was how to provide promised benefits to the soldiers of the Revolution. Finally, the new nation was faced with providing its own defenses and, therefore, having to raise tax monies to equip its navy.

The Americans had to decide how much power to give the state. Having just broken away from a situation in which too much state power had created a threat to liberty, the new nation was very cautious. With the writings of Locke and Smith on their minds, the Americans set out to create an operationally efficient set of property rights.

The Articles of Confederation adopted in 1781 were the first attempt to establish a new institutional order. Because of the excesses of power experienced under King George, the colonists were reluctant to grant the new federal government much discretionary authority. Congress was denied the powers of taxation and regulation of commerce; thus, the amount of resources the national government could control was restricted. But so little power was given to the national government that it was unable to undertake the protective and productive functions demanded at that level. The central government had to rely on state governments to collect taxes imposed by Congress, and the states often acted as free riders. Individual states could impose internal trade barriers, and these diluted many economic benefits of union. Finally, since there was no federal judiciary, uncertainty increased when state courts were called on to enforce national laws.

Although there was little danger of the national government's offering many opportunities for rent seeking, there were also real questions about whether it had enough power to carry out the functions that the citizens desired. Shays' Rebellion, a 1786 uprising against contractual obligations, strengthened the position of those arguing for a stronger central government. As the defects of the Articles became more and more evident, there was a call for a convention. Initially, efforts were aimed at overhauling the Articles of Confederation, but in the end an entirely new framework of national government and legal order was created.

THE CONSTITUTION AND FEDERALIST POLICIES

The new institutional order drew heavily on the colonial heritage, including both the actual property rights structure and the thinking of such writers as Locke and Smith. The Constitution established the framework for the efficient conduct of private economic activities. It defined the protection of private property and the enforcement of contracts, and it created a system of stability. The Constitution's contributions toward establishing a climate of legal and political stability, reducing uncertainty, recognizing the right to private property, and guaranteeing the enforcement of contracts were vital and were conducive to making a market economy work well. An institutional framework had been established that was favorable to economic growth.

In addition to the general theme of limited government and security of private rights, the Constitution and the Bill of Rights embodied some specific guarantees against governmental takings. Three provisions of the basic social contract were particularly important in promoting growth and discouraging rent seeking: (1) article one, section 10, the contract clause; (2) article one, section 8, the commerce clause; and (3) the Fifth Amendment.

1.   The contract clause specified that "no state shall . . . pass any Bill of Attainder, ex post facto law or law impairing the Obligation of Contracts." If the market system is to perform the basic functions of communication, coordination, and motivation, exchange of property rights must be allowed. Freedom of contract is necessary to establish basic stability and predictability so that specialization and exchange can occur. In fact, the government's inability to enforce freedom of

contract under the Articles of Confederation was a major reason for their demise.

2.   The commerce clause was designed as a negative check on the state control of interstate trade. If individual states were allowed to impose duties on goods and interstate commerce, the terms of trade would be artificially altered and the costs of market transactions raised. Furthermore, rent seeking would be encouraged in the form of special trade limitations. Again, the experience under the Articles of Confederation pointed out the importance of not allowing such artificial barriers.

3.   The Fifth Amendment provides that no person shall be "deprived of life, liberty, or property without due process of law." This amendment was a sanctification of the idea of natural rights. Although implicit in the rest of the Constitution, this clause made it clear that the government's ability to alter property rights was constrained by a rule of law.

Other parts of the Constitution were also important for reducing transaction costs and specifying the protective and productive role of the state. The power to levy taxes was delegated to the central government, making it possible to undertake the necessary functions of federal authority. It was now possible to provide public goods, such as national defense and roads. Innovation was encouraged "by securing for limited Times to Authors and Inventors the exclusive Right to their respective Writings and discoveries." Authority over foreign affairs was also given to the federal government, so that tariffs, treaty negotiations, and agreements were no longer at the discretion of individual states. The right to coin money and to regulate its value, another transaction cost reducing measure, was assigned to the federal government.

For promoting economic growth, the most efficient government would be one that attempted to equate private and social benefits and costs and one that would act only where it had an advantage over private organizations in conducting transactions (see Chapter II). Protection of property rights, administration of justice, and provision of defense are activities in which economies of scale and the free rider problem have led to collective action. But we can go further. Given any level of technology (which determines the costs of establishing and enforcing property rights), an efficient Constitution will devise a set of rules to equate the private and social rates of return and to assign to collective action only those activities that can be more efficiently performed by government. It is hard to imagine that the Founding Fathers could have done better on this score. The Constitution, subsequent Federalist enactments, and the decisions of the Marshall-dominated Supreme Court provided a hospitable framework for economic growth in the nineteenth century.

That the Founding Fathers chose a relatively efficient set of rights rather than opting for a rent-seeking society, for which there was ample historical precedent, does not mean that they were not self-interested. Charles Beard, in the *Economic Interpretation of the Constitution*, examined the background of those who dominated the convention and argued that they wrote a Constitution aimed at protecting their own interests. Moreover, since class interests were the basis of their individual actions, he believed that it was essentially a class document. It well may have been that those who were most influential found it to their advantage to institute the rules they did. Regardless of their motives, they did set up an institutional framework that promoted economic growth.

One final point needs to be made. Any document laying out a set of basic rules must be interpreted. It would be difficult, if not impossible, to formulate such rules in a way that would not require interpretation. Therefore, although the Founding Fathers established an efficient set of rights that encouraged a productive society, the continuation of that society depended on the interpretations given to the document.

A LESSON FROM HISTORY:

Is the Majority Always Right?

Any time that a collective body decides to act there must be agreement about the decision rule that is used. The one followed most often is simple majority (50 percent plus one). In fact, in groups in which no explicit rule has been established, almost everyone assumes that action will be taken on the basis of agreement by a simple majority. Although this rule may be best for certain decisions, in some instances a strong case can be made for other rules (unanimity, two-thirds majority, etc.). For example, when basic rights such as freedom of speech, press, and religion are involved, allowing a simple majority to rule can be decidedly inappropriate.

The accompanying three graphs illustrate the economics of decision rules. The horizontal axis on each graph measures the number of individuals from the total, N, necessary for making a collective decision. External costs on the vertical axis in Panel a exist because actions taken by the collective body will not necessarily reflect the preferences of an individual. Furthermore, these costs will decrease throughout because the larger the number of individuals required to take collective action, the more likely that preferences of any single individual will be represented. At N, unanimity, there will be no external costs since the individual can prevent collective action by withholding agreement. Panel b relates decison-making costs to the number of individuals required to take collective action. As the decision rule goes to unanimity, these costs will rise. The optimal or minimum cost decision rule is found by summing these two cost curves (Panel c). Since external costs and decision-making costs will vary depending on the issue, group homogeneity, and so on, the optimal decision rule will vary. If external costs are large relative to decision-making costs, the minimum point will be closer to unanimity. On the other hand, if external costs are low relative to decision-making costs, the optimal rule can be less than simple majority.

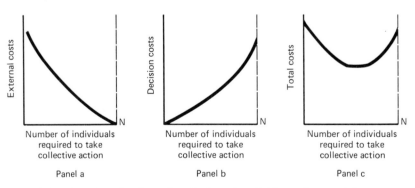

It is clear that the Founding Fathers implicitly understood the economics of decision rules and incorporated this understanding into the Constitution. At one extreme they allowed one-fifth of those present in the House or Senate to enter proceedings in the Congressional Record; at the other, they required complete unanimity before a state could be "deprived of its equal suffrage in the Senate." The Constitution also required more than a simple majority for amendments because they altered the fundamental rules of the society. In the *Federalist Papers* James Madison further expressed concern that a majority might "sacrifice to its ruling passion or interest both the public good and the rights of citizens." Recognizing the economics of decision rules can help us avoid such a "tyranny of the majority."

Suggested Readings:

> Buchanan, James M., and Gordon Tullock, *The Calculus of Consent* (Ann Arbor, Mich.: University of Michigan Press, 1962), Chapter 6.
>
> Hamilton, Alexander, James Madison, and John Jay, *The Federalist Papers* (New York: New American Library, 1961).

VI

American Expansion, 1790–1860

By 1790, the political crisis had been resolved, and the economy was enjoying more prosperity than it had since before the Revolution. With an unlimited supply of rich lands and an energetic populace, prospects for the long run appeared to be excellent. Yet there was no immediate promise of very rapid growth. The reason for this paradox was that the domestic economy was so small and scattered that the home market was very limited, and the foreign market was circumscribed by the Navigation Acts and by the mercantilist policies of the countries with which the new nation dealt.

In 1790 there were less than four million people in the United States, almost 700,000 of whom were slaves. The population was almost evenly divided between North and South, with somewhat more than 200,000 people living in the new western territories. Only 5 percent of the population was urban, and only two cities, New York and Philadelphia, had more than 25,000 residents. This small and scattered population did not provide a very substantial market for expansion. Of that great majority who lived outside the cities, many were not a part of the market, since they neither produced crops for sale nor brought commodities on any regular basis.

We have already observed the vicissitudes of the new nation's foreign trade. Although it expanded and grew from the lean years of the early 1780s, on a per capita basis it was still well below the level it had held in the prosperous years that preceded the Revolution. Since the country was no longer part of the British Empire and was now subject to many mercantilist restrictions, numerous adjustments had to be made. For example, American ships were prohibited from trading directly with the British West Indies; the British fishery in Newfoundland was off limits to American ships; and significant British duties were imposed on American whale oil, all of which in turn affected New England ship building. Thus, the economic outlook for the new nation was not good.

Despite these rather dismal prospects, the period from 1790 to 1860 was characterized by significant economic growth. Real per capita income more than doubled during this period, and extensive growth occurred at a rate of approximately 4 percent per year. A major reason for this rather substantial economic growth was the institutional environment established by the Constitution and strengthened by Supreme Court decisions.

The Constitution established the groundwork for a productive society, but the basic document had to be interpreted (see Chapter V). John Marshall, Chief Justice from 1801 to 1835, provided early interpretations that were important in establishing the incentive structure for the operation of the economy. The decisions of the Marshall Court further strengthened the Constitution by limiting the possibilities for rent seeking.

For the Constitution to serve as an effective limit on government, the Supreme Court had to be able to negate state statutes that contradicted the basic intent of the social contract. Surprisingly enough, the Constitution did not empower any one tribunal to settle disputes arising under the document. From 1789 to 1801, there were numerous disagreements over the appropriate role of federal and state courts. The issue was settled early in Marshall's tenure, and the Supreme Court was given the ultimate authority.

The contract clause of the constitution provided a significant restriction on the power of government to interfere in private economic matters. The Marshall Court interpreted the clause in a manner that encouraged efficiency and growth. Marshall wrote a series of decisions in which he argued that contracts freely entered into were not to be circumscribed by the government. This promoted the stability of property rights and facilitated the movement of resources to their highest-valued use.

The commerce clause also was interpreted in a way that reduced the ability of government to bestow special favors and privileges. Many states were interested in granting monopoly rights to various firms and individuals, and there was ample precedent for this in the mercantilistic doctrines of Europe. But the Supreme Court continually negated such grants under the commerce clause. Thus, freedom of entry was preserved, and entrepreneurial activity was encouraged.

Overall, the Marshall Court established important bulwarks against transfer activity. It protected property rights, limited government to its protective and productive roles, and generally allowed individuals to pursue gains from trade. Thus, the growth pattern from 1790 to 1860 must be understood in the context of the relatively efficient set of rights established by the Constitution and encouraged by the Marshall Court.

AMERICAN EXPANSION IN A WORLD AT WAR

The year 1793 was a doubly significant one in American economic history. Eli Whitney invented the cotton gin and Britain went to war with France, a war that lasted (with one major interruption) until 1815. The cotton gin established cotton as a major crop in the South and a significant source of American economic activity. Britain's war with France more immediately affected our economy. It tied up the shipping and trade of England, France, and most European countries and gave the neutral United States an overwhelming advantage in world trade. At one fell swoop, the restrictions of the Navigation Acts and mercantilist policies were removed from the American carrying trade. The United States transported sugar, coffee, cocoa, pepper, spices, and other commodities from the tropical and subtropical parts of the world to Europe and in turn brought manufactured goods from Europe to the rest of the world. In addition, domestic exports increased, particularly as cotton spread throughout the South and as demand increased from the new cotton textile mills in England (see Figures VI.1 and VI.2).

The expansion of trade and shipping was not accomplished without severe trial and tribulation. Neither side in the war was happy with the role the United States had assumed, and in 1797 and 1798, French seizures of American ships on the one hand and talks of peace on the other led to a decline in shipping activities. Peace came in 1801, and until 1803 there was another precipitous drop in our trading activity as European nations carried their own trade. From 1803 to 1807, the United States experienced another period of turbulent expansion. The end was in sight by 1805, however, when the Essex decision caused the British to revert to a 1756 rule that forbade neutrals from carrying in time of war any goods that had not been carried during time of

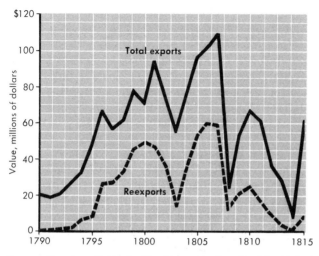

Source: Douglass C. North, *The Economic Growth of the United States, 1790–1860* (Englewood Cliffs, N.J.: Prentice-Hall, Inc., 1961), p. 26.

Figure VI.1 VALUE OF EXPORTS AND REEXPORTS FROM THE UNITED STATES, 1790–1815

Figure VI.2 NET FREIGHT EARNINGS OF UNITED STATES CARRYING TRADE, 1790–1815

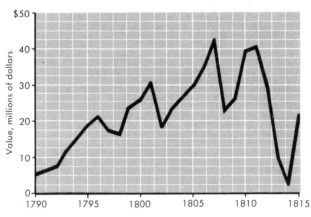

Source: Douglass C. North, *The Economic Growth of the United States, 1790–1860* (Englewood Cliffs, N.J.: Prentice-Hall, Inc., 1961) p. 28.

peace. This rule, combined with Napoleon's Berlin decree attempting to blockade Britain, meant that the end of our lucrative expansion was near. President Thomas Jefferson, fearing that continued shipping would involve the United States in the war, declared an embargo, and in 1808, there was a precipitous decline in trade. Shipping and trade recovered somewhat between 1809 and 1812, although it did not reach the level enjoyed before 1807. With America's entry into the conflict in 1812, the British blockade effectively eliminated most of our external trade.

The period from 1793 to 1807 was a prosperous one for the American economy. There are numerous literary observations of the economy during that time, and we do have some statistics, such as urbanization increasing from 5 to 7.3 percent and rapid expansion of major cities (Baltimore, Boston, New York, and Philadelphia) between 1790 and 1810. A substantial increase in productivity was primarily the result of the growth in the market. That growth, in turn, was stimulated as the relatively high prices being paid for our exports (see Figure VI.3) attracted America's agricultural products into the marketplace and made it possible for farmers to specialize, thereby pulling them out of self-sufficiency and into the market economy. Moreover, the temporary phenomenon of high export prices coupled with low import prices (reflecting the situation of a world at war) meant, at least for a brief period, that the country was better off than ever before. We were able to buy more manufactured imports with every dollar of exports.[1]

With the embargo, prosperity came to an end, and 1808 was characterized by depression and unemployment that reached the seacoast and the market-oriented sectors of the American economy. Despite some relaxation of the embargo, with subsequent acts designed to stimulate trade with one or another of the belligerents, the United States never completely recovered in the years 1808 to 1812, and much of the capital that businessmen had invested in shipping was channeled into manufacturing. The embargo meant not only that we did not sell to belligerents; we could not buy from them either. As a result, the prices of manufactured goods rose dramatically, encouraging businessmen to put their capital where the profits were. Consequently, where before 1808 only fifteen cotton mills had been built in the United States, by the end of 1809 there were eighty-seven additional mills; and this ex-

---

[1] One cannot attribute all of the increase in per capita income to the improvement in the terms of trade, however. Claudia D. Goldin and Frank D. Lewis, "The Role of Exports in American Economic Growth During the Napoleonic Wars, 1793 to 1807," *EEH*, 17 (January, 1980), estimate that only between 25 and 40 percent of the increase was the result of American neutrality.

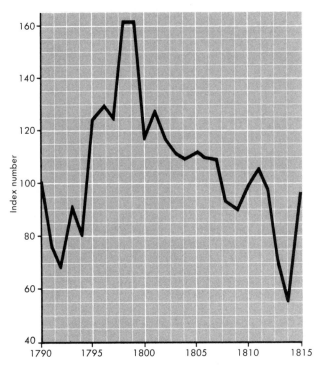

Source: Douglass C. North, *The Economic Growth of the United States 1790–1860* (Englewood Cliffs, N.J.: Prentice-Hall, Inc., 1961), p. 31.

Figure VI.3   U.S. TERMS OF TRADE, 1790–1815

pansion continued right up through the War of 1812. Similar activity in manufacturing increased domestic production of formerly imported goods.

It is clear that American capital at that time would have been more profitably employed if it could have been used in shipping, with the earning from that shipping used to buy British manufactures. The British, with their relatively cheaper capital and skilled labor, could produce goods more inexpensively than we could. By the same token, we enjoyed advantages in shipping. But the embargo had forced us to take an inefficient course. American manufacturing developed prematurely, thriving only under the artificial protection of the embargo and the war. When the War of 1812 ended, England's more efficiently produced exports turned into shattering competition, and there was a drastic decline in American manufacturing.

Even during the years 1808 to 1814, the economy was less prosperous than it had been prior to the embargo. In addition to the less efficient use of resources between 1808 and 1814, there was substantial unemployment and the dislocation of economic activity that accompanied America's involvement in the war.

THE ECONOMY AFTER THE SECOND WAR WITH ENGLAND

In 1815, when America emerged from its second war with England, its position was somewhat analogous to that of 1790. The United States was still a newcomer among the nations of the world. Although its population had increased from not quite 4,000,000 in 1790 to about 8,400,000 in 1815, the citizenry was still scattered. Approximately half of the population lived in the North and half in the South, and more than one million adventurous souls had moved across the Appalachian Mountains and settled in the New West. Many of these settlers had come in the wake of Lewis and Clark's expedition in 1803, which gave evidence of untold prospects for growth in the lands acquired in the Louisiana Purchase at the beginning of the nineteenth century.

The vast, promising, unsettled reaches of the West added assets of unknown value to the scattered settlement up and down the east coast of the United States. But another aspect of the economy had changed little since 1790: our relationship to foreign countries. The things we did best—shipping and exporting agricultural commodities—were circumscribed by the navigation laws and by the mercantilist policies that still dominated most of Europe. Our international trade seemed to be reverting to the kinds of restrictions it faced in 1790, but there was one significant difference.

When Eli Whitney invented the cotton gin in 1793, he changed the face of the South. The cotton gin became the mainspring of the Southern economy. It encouraged the perpetuation of slavery, thus ultimately helping to promote the conflict that was to engulf America in 1861. Cotton became the crucial export commodity for much of the South and the major source of cash income for many farmers. Exceptions were coastal South Carolina, where rice was the major crop; southern Louisiana, where sugar cane was dominant; and the upper South, where tobacco was gradually giving way to more diversified farming. Even in the states dominated by cotton production, the seasonal nature of the crop meant that the additional costs of producing foodstuffs were relatively low, making the South self-sufficient in food. Nevertheless, cotton was a major force in the economy, and world cotton demand played a dynamic role in the economic fortunes of the South.

In examining the influence of cotton on the economy, we should recall that Jefferson's embargo sent a good deal of dispossessed American capital and other resources into manufacturing. Production of cotton textiles, machinery, and equipment expanded so rapidly between 1808 and 1814 that many people optimistically thought that industrialization was an accomplished fact. We know now that a peacetime economy revealed our inadequacies. Bankruptcies spread as English textiles and other manufactured products flooded into the United States and effectively undersold the more expensive locally produced goods. Clearly, America did not have Britain's manufacturing efficiency and was not yet ready to claim any birthright as a manufacturing nation. Basically, the period of the early 1800s was one of readjustment for American industry.

The early nineteenth century found the South exporting its cotton to England. At the time, Britain was in the midst of the Industrial Revolution, and the major products of the new factory system were cotton textiles. A growing demand for raw cotton naturally resulted, and America, more than any other country in the world, was able to meet the demand. Whenever supply did not keep up with demand, cotton prices soared, and planters put more of their acreage into cotton.

The spread of the cotton economy in the South and the development of the cotton export trade are the elements of a well-known story. It now appears, however, that economic historians have overemphasized the pattern of regional interdependence among the South, the West, and the Northeast. There *was* considerable trade among these regions, but it is an oversimplification to suggest that the South produced only cotton, the West only foodstuffs, and the Northeast only manufactured goods and shipping services. Perhaps more important was the intraregional specialization that was occurring. As transportation costs fell and as markets developed, specialization on a local level increased. Farmers found it to their advantage not to be as diversified as they had been. Some members of the economy discovered that they had a comparative advantage in providing certain services, and local manufacturers specialized and expanded their production.

Intraregional specialization coupled with interregional trade produced economic growth throughout the period. From the beginning of the cotton trade, the Northeast had provided shipping and insurance and had gradually found a growing market for manufactures in the South and West. As it became a deficit food area, the Northeast received foodstuffs from the West, at first via the Mississippi and by coastal vessels to eastern ports, and later (especially after the 1840s) via the Great Lakes and the Erie Canal. Since cotton textiles were a major part of eastern manufactures, cotton exports to the Northeast were also a growing part of this regionally interdependent relationship.[2]

REGIONAL SPECIALIZATION AND DEVELOPMENT

The behavior of prices decided how development in the South was to take place. Figure VI.4 shows the prices of cotton in relation to the sales of lands in the new Southwest (Arkansas, Louisiana, Mississippi, Alabama, and Florida). Note the coincidence between periods of high prices and periods of high sales of these new lands. In each period, higher prices for agricultural commodities (in this case, cotton) lured planters with their slaves into the new, fertile land in search of high returns from cotton cultivation. (The same pattern applied to the West, with different kinds of commodities.) Therefore, expansion in the South during this period was induced by the growing demand for cotton in Europe, which led to rising prices, to surges of expansion into the Southwest, and to an ever-increasing supply of cotton. The British helped to finance this expansion by making loans to banks in Louisiana and Mississippi; the banks, in turn, financed planters' opening up new lands.

Although there had been some early western settlement soon after the Revolutionary War, the opening of a far-reaching transportation network stimulated a much greater westward movement. The first link was forged from the Mississippi, the Missouri, and the Ohio. Along these waters and their tributaries, the western products could flow to the South and then to the Northeast or to foreign markets. Later, canals opened other parts of the West and, even more important, connected the whole region with the East Coast—with construction again financed in part by British capital.

The West was able to produce remuneratively both cereals and commodities derived from cereals. Wheat, corn, and livestock products were the mainstays of the western economy. As decades wore on and

---

[2] The importance of early tariff legislation in the revival of manufacturing has been a much-debated subject. The acts of 1816, 1824, and 1828 all provided protection and with the fall in prices after 1818 were probably important in the revival of some branches of the textile industry, but by 1830 the United States was exporting textiles and was able to stand on its own feet. In addition, the high transportation costs into the interior provided protection for the early iron industry in western Pennsylvania between 1820 and 1837.

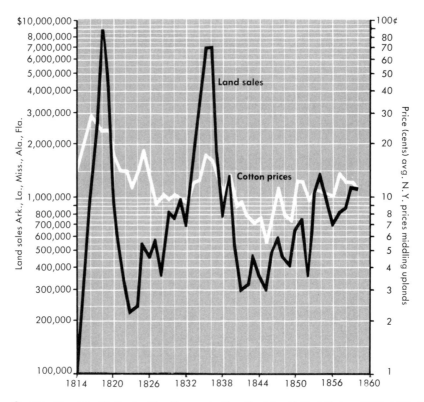

Source: Douglass C. North, *The Economic Growth of the United States, 1790–1860* (Englewood Cliffs, N.J.: Prentice-Hall, Inc., 1961) p. 124.

Figure VI.4 PUBLIC LAND SALES AND COTTON PRICES, 1814–1860

better transportation facilities became available, a growing demand expanded the direct movement of these goods to the East.

The West was more diversified than the South. For example, lead was found in Missouri, and a substantial downriver trade developed as ore was carried to New Orleans for export. Similarly, copper in Michigan and iron ore in western Pennsylvania produced early patterns of mining activity, and the iron industry flourished in western Pennsylvania, southern Ohio, and northern Kentucky. Thus while the South concentrated on agricultural production, the West reached out into a broader range of economic activity.

A familiar pattern emerges when wheat and corn prices are compared with sales of land in seven western states (see Figure VI.5). As with southern cotton, rising wheat prices induced mass movement into the rich lands of Ohio, Illinois, Indiana, Michigan, Iowa, Wisconsin, and Missouri. Output of western agricultural goods responded to price increases induced by the growing demand from the East and from Europe (beginning with the Irish famine in 1844–46). With an expanding transportation network, the West was able to realize its potential in a pattern of interregional trade based on market-oriented production. The West—already more diversified than the South—was destined to become a more broadly based economy in which manufacturing would later develop.

In 1820, the Northeast was recovering from its abortive industrialization, which had been crushed by British competition. The area still depended on commerce, shipping, and agriculture. In fact, even though declining in significance, the shipping and commerce sector continued to be an important source of income in the Northeast throughout the nineteenth century. This was especially true between 1815 and 1860. American ships and their goods were trading all over

Figure VI.5   LAND SALES IN SEVEN WESTERN STATES, 1815 –1860

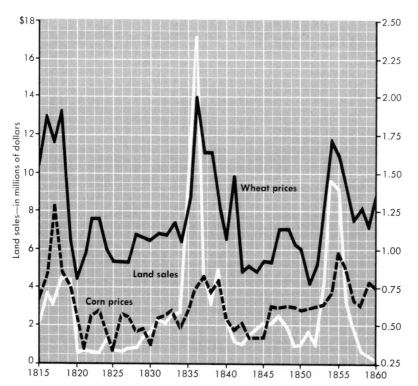

Source: Douglass C. North, *Economic Growth of the United States, 1790–1860*, (Englewood
    Cliffs, N.J.: Prentice-Hall, Inc., 1961), p. 137.

the world, and the merchants of Boston, Salem, and other East Coast ports were active in trade from China and India to Africa and all parts of Europe. Agriculture, fishing, and whaling continued in the nineteenth century to hold an important place in the Northeast's economy.

The most interesting and significant development between 1815 and 1860 was the increasing productivity throughout the economy. Merchants continually sought more efficient ways to market both agricultural commodities and manufactured goods. These innovations lowered transaction costs and, although not usually considered part of technological change, were responsible for significant gains in productivity. In the South, for example, cotton brokers, or factors, took over many of the marketing functions. In addition to buying the crop from the farmer and selling it abroad, the factor provided insurance and banking services. Transaction costs were also lowered by improving the information system. Agricultural fairs gave farmers a ready source of information about new techniques, breeds, and varieties. Newspaper distribution and specialized publications increased rapidly. These developments, together with a decline in transportation costs (see Chapter IX), integrated markets, allowed economies of scale to be realized, and served to pinpoint potential mutual gains from production and trade.

One of the most obvious forms of specialization in production between 1815 and 1860 was the gradual and then the vigorous revival of manufacturing. It began with a slow stirring in the 1820s. Then, in the 1830s, manufacturing—particularly of cotton textiles—rapidly gained momentum in southern New England, in New York, and to a lesser extent in Pennsylvania. Concurrently with the growth of textiles, the iron industry, machinery production, and a variety of other manufactures also evolved, reflecting the beginning of diversified manufacturing activity.

There were essentially two kinds of manufacturing in 1860: resource industries and light manufacturing (see Table VI.1). Resource industries dealt in the processing of resources, such as the production of flour and cornmeal from wheat and corn. This was a substantial part of northeastern manufacturing and was typically developed at geographical locations where grain from the farms was brought for transshipment. Lumbering was another important resource-oriented industry.

Light manufacturing included cotton goods; boots and shoes, men's clothing, leather, and woolen goods; and machinery. A broad pattern of manufacturing had evolved in the Northeast by 1860, with cotton textiles in the vanguard. The Waltham Mills was a pioneer in this industry. It was established in Massachusetts in 1813 during the second war with England. The flood of English textiles that followed

TABLE VI.1   Leading Branches of Manufacturing in the United States, 1860

Rank by Value Added	Item	Value Added (millions of $)	Number of Establishments	Employment per Establishment
1	Cotton goods	55	803	143
2	Lumber	54	20,165	4
3	Boots and shoes	49	12,486	10
4	Iron	46	2,252	30
5	Clothing	41	4,209	29
6	Flour and meal	40	13,868	2
7	Machinery	33	1,388	30
8	Leather	26	5,188	5
9	Woolen goods	25	1,227	33
10	Liquors	22	2,741	7

Source: U.S Census Bureau, *Eighth Census of the United States, 1860 Manufacturers* (Washington: GPO, 1865), pp. 733–42.

the peace treaty of 1814 did not bankrupt the Waltham Mills, as it did many other textile firms. The Waltham Mills succeeded primarily because of large-scale production and the manufacturing of coarse sheeting, a cheap and simple cotton cloth that a frontier, pioneering society could use in all kinds of finished cotton textile goods. In addition, the English power loom was adapted to American needs and put to work in the Waltham Mills (foreshadowing the continual modification of British technology to fit American conditions). Thus, with the efficient, large-scale production of low grade cotton fabric, a mill was established, managed to survive, and actually did rather well. Although the Waltham Mills was exceptional, the conditions for other manufacturing expansion were gradually becoming more favorable.

Several cautionary notes are in order here. The rise of the factory systems did not mean a move to large-scale production in the sense that we think of it today. The average number of employees per establishment was relatively small (again, see Table VI.1). Only in cotton goods did factory size approach what might today be considered a large manufacturing firm. The small number of employees per firm meant that there were a large number of firms. For instance, 12,500 manufacturing establishments produced boots and shoes. But despite the small size and large number of firms, manufacturing still represented a dramatic shift in the forms of production. At the turn of the century, most manufacturing was carried out in the home. Movement to a workplace where individuals were engaged in manufacturing a common product represented a substantial change.

New organizational forms of production appear to have resulted in technological change rather than to have been the cause of it. The standard interpretation of the rise of manufacturing argues that inventions created the economies of scale that led to the factory system. It seems more likely that the move toward central workshops was an effort to secure greater quality control in the production process. The organizational changes were necessary to improve the monitoring of workers, and once production was centralized, the cost of devising technical improvements was reduced. Productivity gains from team production became more evident, and the benefits from devising machines to replace workers were more obvious. Thus, the direction of change was not from technological innovation to the factory system, but from the development of the central work place to supervision to more specialization to better measurement of input contributions and finally to technological change. Also, much of the technological change that occurred because of the new organizational systems was incremental.

Another important factor in creating the alterations in technology was the marriage of science and technology. Although the importance of science to technological change accelerated in the last part of the nineteenth century, its influence was certainly felt before 1860. The development of scientific disciplines, the rapid exchange of information among all parts of society, and the increase in general educational levels contributed to this change. Engineers, craftsmen, and

TABLE VI.2   International Comparison of Relative School
Populations, 1850

	Ratio of Students to Total Population
New England	25.71%
Denmark	21.73
U.S. (excluding slaves)	20.40
Sweden	17.85
Saxony	16.66
Prussia	16.12
Norway	14.28
Belgium	12.04
Great Britain (on the books)	11.76
Great Britain (in attendance Mar. 31, 1851)	14.28
France	9.52
Austria	7.29
Holland	6.99
Ireland	6.89
Greece	5.55
Russia	2.00
Portugal	1.22

Source: U.S. Census Bureau. *A Compendium of the Seventh Census,* J.D.B. DeBow, Superintendent of Census (Washington: GPO, 1854), p. 148.

technicians adapted and modified British techniques for American use. Informal and formal education were comparatively common (see Table VI.2). Human capital accumulation provided the essential skilled labor force that was so important to obtaining high levels of productivity in both manufacturing and agriculture.

SOURCES OF EXPANSION

We have detailed numerous changes in the economy that contributed to the growth in per capita and aggregate income between 1790 and 1860. There was intra- and interregional specialization throughout the period. There were frequent organizational innovations in production and in marketing. New products were produced, and cheaper methods were found for manufacturing old ones. In addition, people were investing in themselves at a rapid rate. Savings were substantial, and capital markets were becoming rapidly integrated. Transaction costs were sharply reduced in most of the economy.

Although at one time or another economic historians have labeled each of these contributors to growth as "crucial," emphasizing any one or any combination ignores the more fundamental issue of why and how such changes occurred. Each change in the economy was the result of individual decision making based on personal calculations of costs and benefits. For those changes to have occurred, the institutional environment had to be one in which individuals were encouraged to take those actions. A relatively efficient rights structure promoted a vast array of creative activity. Well-defined and -enforced property rights led people to seek out new organizational frameworks that promised economic gain, to invest in their own skills and training, to obey the law of comparative advantage, to save and loan to others who promised a high rate of return on investment, and to search for new products and services.

It is important that the human element not be ignored in all of these decisions. As noted previously, there were 12,500 manufacturers of boots and shoes in 1860. That meant that 12,500 people saw the potential for making a profit from setting up the appropriate organizational form, attracting inputs from competing uses, and developing markets for their product. Similar entrepreneurial decisions were being made in all sectors of the economy. As a result, the country experienced what James Willard Hurst has called the "release of energy." Of course, not all entrepreneurs were successful, but the incentives were there for them to seek out potential gains from trade.

VII

The Economy of the South, 1800–1914

The economy of the South was a subject of seemingly endless controversy during the nineteenth century, and the controversy persists. The fact of slavery and a subsequent century in which racial issues have dominated the political, social, and economic climate have made scientific analysis difficult. The efforts of new economic historians relying on economic theory, however, have provided us with an approach that has resolved many issues. Three books stand out and form the basis for much of our discussion. The first, *Time on the Cross*, by Robert Fogel and Stanley Engerman,[1] is devoted to analyzing slavery in the antebellum South. The authors' conclusions regarding efficiency and exploitation have sparked many arguments among historians and economists and have helped focus the debate over slavery. Gavin Wright, in *The Political Economy of the Cotton South*,[2] places more emphasis on the overall economic conditions in the South. He expands our understanding of the production process, including the institution of slavery. Finally, the work of Roger Ransom and Richard Sutch, *One Kind of Freedom*,[3] addresses many new issues about the economic sys-

[1] Robert William Fogel and Stanley L. Engerman, *Time on the Cross*, (Boston: Little Brown and Company, 1974).

[2] Gavin Wright, *The Political Economy of the Cotton South* (New York: W.W. Norton and Company, Inc., 1978).

[3] Roger Ransom and Richard Sutch, *One Kind of Freedom* (New York: Cambridge University Press, 1977).

tem in which the freed slaves found themselves after the Civil War. Many questions are still to be answered, and many issues remain controversial, but the application of theory has focused the debate and provided systematic analysis.

THE ANTEBELLUM ECONOMY

In the years preceding the Civil War, the South concentrated heavily on the production of a few staple commodities to sell outside the region. Cotton was by far the most important, although rice in South Carolina, sugar in Louisiana, and tobacco in the upper South were also significant export commodities. In addition to producing for export, the South was basically self-sufficient in the production of foodstuffs. Corn was produced in such large quantities for feeding slaves and livestock that in some years the value of the corn crop exceeded the combined value of cotton, tobacco, sugar, and rice. In 1849, corn covered 18 million acres in the South while cotton covered only 5 million acres; and in 1860, 28 percent of all Southern farms produced no cotton.[4]

The plantation economy used large amounts of land and large amounts of labor. In the new South, the size of plantations was substantial, running to hundreds and sometimes thousands of acres. Slaves, of course, supplied the labor and constituted the major capital investment in the plantation system. Between 1802 and 1860, the nominal price of prime fieldhands rose from $600 to about $1,800. The increase in slave prices merely reflected their increasing value in commodity production.

A salient feature of the Southern system was the rich, western land that was available for extensive expansion of cotton culture. Between 1815 and 1860, planters and slaves moved westward in a series of surges that led to rapid population growth in the new Southwest (see Table VII.1). The main surge occurred between 1833 and 1837, although land sales in the latter part of the 1850s did increase modestly. There were several important differences between plantations in the older areas (the Carolinas and Georgia) and those in the new Southwest. Plantations in the older areas had higher production costs of cotton and were less specialized, whereas the new plantations— particularly those in Louisiana and Mississippi—tended to be highly concentrated in large-scale production of cotton or sugar.

Although we often classify the South as a plantation economy,

---

[4] Wright, *The Cotton South*, p. 18.

TABLE VII.1 Population of Free (Black and White) and Slaves of Alabama, Arkansas, Florida, Louisiana, and Mississippi, 1820–1860

	1820	1830	1840	1850	1860
Ala.					
F	86,622	191,978	337,224	428,779	529,121
S	41,879	117,549	253,532	342,892	435,080
Ark.					
F	12,638	25,812	77,639	162,797	324,335
S	1,617	4,576	19,935	47,100	111,115
Fla.					
F	—	19,229	28,760	48,135	78,680
S	—	15,501	25,717	39,309	61,745
La.					
F	83,857	106,251	183,959	272,953	376,276
S	69,064	109,588	168,452	244,809	331,726
Miss.					
F	42,634	70,962	180,440	296,698	354,674
S	32,814	65,659	195,211	309,878	436,631
Total (F and S)	371,125	727,105	1,470,869	2,193,300	3,039,383

Source: U.S. Congress, House *Preliminary Report on the Eighth Census, 1860* (Washington GPO, 1862), pp. 126–33.

the majority of Southern whites did not own slaves. A high proportion of Southern whites lived on small farms, and many were only peripherally connected to the market. In 1860, 50 percent of the farms operated with no slaves.[5] Furthermore, the top 10 percent of wealthholders in the cotton South owned 57 percent of the wealth, produced 68 percent of the cotton, and owned 61 percent of all slaves.[6] These figures suggest that a substantial portion of the population did not live on large plantations.

This does not suggest, however, that King Cotton did not determine the growth pattern in the antebellum South. The comparative advantage of cotton over alternative products was so great that it was the rational investment for the Southerner to make. In the few years around 1845, cotton's decline in price to five cents per pound was viewed as temporary. In general, the Southerner correctly believed that his income would be higher from cotton production than it would be if he devoted his slaves, his land, and his other resources to an alternative economic activity. This attention to profits and other similar characteristics of the South indicate a wealth-maximizing economy in which people acted rationally. Rising returns from cotton production as a result of rising prices led to the growing westward movement (see

[5] *Ibid.*, p. 18.
[6] *Ibid.*, pp. 25–27.

Figure VI.4). Indeed, westward expansion was induced by the rising returns from commodities that were in demand in the rest of the United States and in the world beyond.

The behavior of cotton prices (Figure VI.4) was governed by the following sequence of events: A period of relatively high cotton prices brought a surge of planters and slaves into the new Southwest. For three or four years, land was cleared, and a preliminary corn crop was sometimes planted. Then, when the land was ready, cotton was planted. As its supply substantially increased, the price of cotton fell drastically until it was no longer an inducement to westward expansion. As a result, some of the land was switched to corn. Cotton prices tended to remain low for a rather lengthy period, however. Any increase in demand was met by a further increase in supply, since planters who had cleared the land could shift from corn back to cotton if it became more profitable to do so. This continued until demand increased enough to employ all the cleared lands; then prices rose.

The adherence to the law of comparative advantage and the efficiency of Southern agriculture did generate economic growth in the South. Per capita income was 25 percent below the national average when slaves are included in the population (see Table VII.2). Excluding slaves, however, the Southern income level exceeded the national average. Moreover, the trend over this period suggests that the per capita income, far from being stagnant, was growing faster than the national average. Between 1840 and 1860, per capita incomes grew at a rate of 39 percent for the total population and 43 percent for the free population.

TABLE VII.2   Personal Income Per Capita in Each Region as Percentage of U.S. Average, 1840–1950 (U.S. = 100)

Regions	1840	1860	1880	1900	1920	1930	1940	1950
NORTHEAST	135	139	141	137	132	138	124	115
New England	132	143	141	134	124	129	121	109
Mid-Atlantic	136	137	141	139	134	140	124	116
NORTH CENTRAL	68	68	98	103	100	101	103	106
E. No. Central	67	69	102	106	108	111	112	112
W. No. Central	75	66	90	97	87	82	84	94
SOUTH	76	72	51	51	62	55	65	73
So. Atlantic	70	65	45	45	59	56	69	74
E. So. Central	73	68	51	49	52	48	55	62
W. So. Central	144	115	60	61	72	61	70	80
WEST			190	163	122	115	125	114
Mountain			168	139	100	83	92	96
Pacific			204	163	135	130	138	121

Source: Richard A. Easterlin, "Regional Income Trends, 1840–1950," *American Economic History*, Seymour E.H. Harris, ed., (New York: McGraw-Hill, 1961), p. 528.

THE SYSTEM OF SLAVERY

Objective analysis of the slavery system is difficult because of the generally accepted immorality of human bondage. For many, it is difficult to accept that such an immoral institution might have been efficient or profitable. Nonetheless, the economic way of thinking gives us a method that provides answers to many of the nagging questions arising out of slavery without at the same time condoning it. We shall confine ourselves to four questions: (1) was slavery profitable; (2) was slavery viable; (3) was slavery efficient; and (4) to what extent did slavery exploit the slaves?

New economic historians have approached the system of slavery as a capital investment. As such, it assumes that the rational plantation owner made decisions on the basis of his perceived net present value of the asset. While this may seem to be a "nonhuman" way of examining a human institution, it is the best way to explain the behavior of Southern slave owners. From this perspective, it is easier to understand the kinds of diet, clothing, and shelter that owners might have provided for their assets. If one thinks of how a modern farmer might approach the decision to purchase and use a tractor, the same kind of decision regarding slaves becomes much clearer. By the same token, the capital investment approach allows us to better understand why measured output might be much higher on slave plantations than on free farms. The owner of a capital asset can obtain benefits from that asset only through production. Therefore, offering leisure time to slaves is rational only insofar as that leisure increases the output from work time. For the free person, however, leisure itself is a good to be traded off against work. In other words, when one owns oneself, narrowly defined income or wealth will not be the only things to be maximized. Slaves were not given much choice over their consumption of leisure or, for that matter, their consumption of many other goods.

From the capital investment perspective, it is not surprising that slavery was profitable. Alfred Conrad and John Meyer, who wrote perhaps the first new economic history, have shown that slave markets were very closely related to capital markets.[7] They conclude that the average return to investing in male slaves was about 6 percent, indicating that the rate of return in slavery was about the same as in other investments. If capital markets were working, this conclusion is not surprising. In a capital market, asset prices will adjust upward or downward until the rate of return approximates that of other invest-

[7] Alfred H. Conrad and John R. Meyer, "The Economics of Slavery in the Antebellum South," *JPE* (April, 1958).

ments. The findings of Robert Fogel and Stanley Engerman further support Conrad and Meyer's conclusion (see Figure VII.1). Prices of young slaves, who faced a higher probability of dying, required more care, and produced less, had to be below the price of prime fieldhands if the investment was to be profitable.

These data tell us that slavery was profitable, but they do not tell us about its expected viability. Many historians have argued that the Civil War was unneccessary because slavery was a moribund institution that would have disappeared anyway. To test this hypothesis, Fogel and Engerman developed an index of sanguinity to measure expectations by comparing the long-run asset price of slaves with the

Figure VII.1   PRICES OF SLAVES BY AGE AND SEX ABOUT 1850, IN THE OLD SOUTH

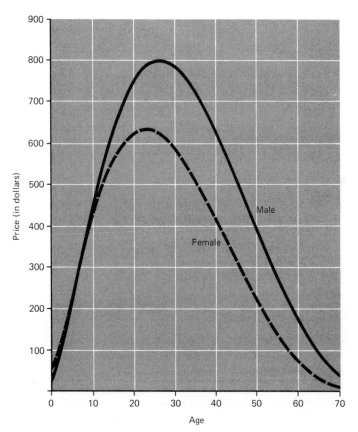

Source: Robert William Fogel and Stanley L. Engerman, *Time on the Cross*, (Boston: Little, Brown and Company, 1974), p. 76.

short-run rental price (see Figure VII.2). This measure captures slave-holders' expectations about the long-run prospects for slave ownership relative to the income produced by a slave in the short term. If slavery had been a dying institution, Southerners would have been less interested in owning slaves, thus putting downward pressure on slave prices. At the same time, however, Southerners would have remained interested in renting slaves on a short-term basis. Had slavery been dying, the combination of these two would have caused the asset price to decline relative to the rental cost. The Fogel and Engerman index shows no such trend, suggesting that Southerners expected slavery to remain viable.

Since slavery was profitable and viable, it is hardly surprising that the institution was also efficient. Fogel and Engerman again provide the supporting data. Their efficiency index shows that compared with Northern farms, free farms in the old South were as efficient, slave farms in the old South were 20 percent more efficient, and slave farms in the new South were 50 percent more efficient. One explanation for this is the opportunity for capturing economies of scale. For all of the cotton states, total factor productivity on farms with one to

Figure VII.2 INDEX OF THE SANGUINITY OF SLAVEHOLDERS, 1830–1860

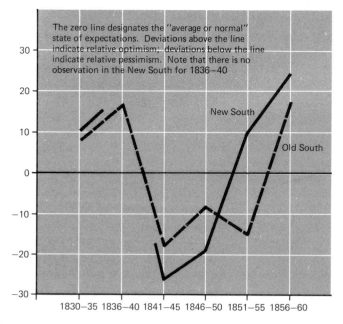

Source: Robert William Fogel and Stanley L. Engerman, *Time on the Cross*, (Boston: Little, Brown and Company, 1974), p. 104.

fifteen slaves, sixteen to fifty slaves, and more than fifty slaves was 8 percent, 45 percent, and 33 percent greater, respectively, than on farms with no slaves. Gavin Wright, however, has correctly pointed out that the efficiency data are clouded by the fact that slaveholders maximized income from cotton production while small free farm owners included leisure and security in their decisions. With less leisure per laborer and more emphasis on cotton production, it is not surprising that measured efficiency was greater on large cotton farms.[8]

The final issue is how badly the slaves were exploited. In one sense, the degree of exploitation cannot be measured, since slavery gave few choices to the blacks. On the other hand, if we consider the extent to which food, shelter, clothing, and medical care offset the total output of slaves, we can get some idea of economic exploitation. To measure economic exploitation, Fogel and Engerman calculate that on average at birth the difference between the discounted value of lifetime output and the discounted value of lifetime maintenance costs was $32. Dividing this by the present value of lifetime output at birth ($265) produces a 12 percent rate of exploitation. This surprisingly low figure is due to two things. First, the Fogel–Engerman technique necessitates offsetting rearing costs in the early years of a slave's life with future output. In the discounting process, this means that the costs receive a relatively higher weight in the calculation. Second, since their technique uses the average for all slaves, the output of those slaves who complete their life cycle must not only be offset against their maintenance costs, it must also be offset against the maintenance costs of those slaves who die at an early age.

To avoid these two factors, Roger Ransom and Richard Sutch, in *One Kind of Freedom*, measure exploitation by subtracting from the average output per slave the cost of slave consumption, capital, land, and management. For 1859, they find that the average value of the total output per slave on all farms was $127.55. Then, subtracting capital, land, and management costs yields a product of labor of $62.46. Since slave consumption amounted to only $28.95, the Ransom and Sutch estimate of exploitation in 1859 exceeds 50 percent.

One way to reconcile these vastly different estimates is to realize that the Fogel and Engerman technique measures exploitation from the slaveholder's viewpoint, and the Ransom and Sutch technique measures it from the slave's viewpoint. It is not possible to say which estimate is better, since the two measure different things. It is clear from either measure, however, that slaveholders had something to lose from emancipation and that slaves had something to gain.

[8] Wright, *The Cotton South*, Chapter 3.

The slavery issue is important because it illustrates both the usefulness and the limits of economic theory. Viewing slavery as an efficient capital market is helpful in understanding the influence of that set of rights on economic growth. The evidence indicates that slavery was a relatively efficient institution in terms of measured economic output. However, economics does not lend much insight into the appropriate distribution of rights. Property rights structures can have very different ownership patterns and still be efficient in the sense of equating private and social rates of return. The question of who should possess what rights is an ethical one that cannot be resolved by an appeal to economic reasoning. It took the Civil War to determine whether a redistribution would take place. The basic structure of property rights, however, was altered very little by the war; only the distribution of human capital ownership was changed.

THE POSTBELLUM ECONOMY

The Civil War was perhaps the first war that resulted in vast military mortality as well as the widespread destruction of capital and natural resources. Sheridan's and Sherman's celebrated marches were only episodes in the sweeping destruction of capital and labor that accompanied the defeat of the South. As significant as the destruction was the fact that the war transformed a mass of capital equipment into 4 million human beings who could choose within the narrow limits of their knowledge and experience between leisure and labor, between city and countryside. Emancipation in fact meant something less than complete freedom, but it is important to understand the magnitude of the potential transformation. Except for the war itself, the abolition of slavery did not entail any change in the total assets of society. But there was a gigantic redistribution of wealth when emancipation was realized.

In comparing the pre- and post–Civil War estimates of economic growth, two factors must be taken into account. First, the Civil War did result in the very real destruction of material and human capital. This in turn reduced the productive capacity of the Southern economy. Second, the transformation of blacks from capital to labor meant that blacks were free to use their time for other than market production. Although this free choice, particularly of leisure, showed up as reduced output, it did not necessarily suggest a lower standard of living. It is not surprising, then, that commodity output per capita in the South between 1860 and 1870 declined by nearly 30 percent while commodity output per capita in the North and West rose by 9 percent. From 1870 to 1890, the rates of increase were slightly more than 20 percent from the South, the North, and the West. Between 1880 and 1900, per capita income grew as rapidly in the South as in the rest of the country, and in the next twenty years per capita income grew more rapidly in the South than anywhere else.

We must get behind the figures in order to understand the Southern economy after the war. By 1880, in most respects physical output in Southern agriculture had recovered to its 1860 level (exceptions were the number of swine and acres in farms); but the *value* of Southern agricultural output was still below the 1860 level. On the other hand, industrial output shows a substantial increase both in number of manufacturing establishments and in capital. Indeed, even the 1870 industrial output figures exceeded those of before the Civil War.[9] After 1880, manufacturing grew substantially in the South. By 1910, there were two-thirds as many cotton spindles in the South as there were in the North, and much of the growth was financed with Northern funds. But the cotton textile industry was not the only beneficiary of Northern capital. Economic theory implies that given relatively scarce capital and abundant labor in the South, capital would flow into all kinds of activity. And that is precisely what happened. Textiles, iron and steel production, and cotton plantations were only some of the beneficiaries. Traditional descriptions of the postbellum South have suggested a long era of stagnation in which Northern capital exploited and kept the South in bondage. This implies that the North delayed Southern economic development. Both assumptions are in error.

[9] Eugene Lerner, "Southern Output and Agricultural Income, 1860–1880," *The Economic Impact of the American Civil War*, R. Andreano, ed., (Cambridge: Schenkman, 1967), p. 110.

A LESSON FROM HISTORY:

Did Early American Farmers Waste Our Land?

Today there is a rising tide of concern that we are wasting resources in general and wasting our agricultural land in particular. A recent National Agricultural Land Survey concluded that development during the 1970s was eroding our agricultural land base at a rate of three million acres per year. Furthermore, it is alleged that tons of topsoil are being eroded from prime Midwestern farmlands.

Such concern for "land butchery" is not without historical precedent. Historians long have chastised colonial and pre-Civil War farmers for their wasteful use of land and timber resources. "Rape and run" tactics of farmers, timber harvesters, and miners are often cited as reason for nonmarket controls of resources.

The economic way of thinking about waste, however, suggests that early agricultural techniques were much more efficient than commonly believed. "Economic waste of land" implies that it is used in ways that have less value than alternatives. With respect to colonial farmers, the counterfactual proposition is that society would have received more value from land preservation than from rapid exploitation during the early years.

To test this hypothesis it is first important to understand that efficient use of land depends on its scarcity relative to other factors of production. During the early years of our nation, land and natural resources in general were relatively abundant while labor and capital were scarce. Agricultural techniques that conserved on the latter and made extensive use of the former allowed output to be produced at minimum cost. European farmers during this period practiced land conservation because land was their relatively scarce factor. Had American farmers followed the same conservation practices, they would have been guilty of wasting valuable labor and capital.

In addition to relative scarcity, the discounted value of land is important for determining whether it was wasted by farmers. Conserving land generally means foregoing present economic returns. Since future returns are discounted, conservation will pay only if it enhances the future value of land. If the discount rate in 1790 were 5 percent, conservation would have to yield more than a 5 percent return to induce the farmer to preserve soil fertility. Putting it differently, with a discount rate of 5 percent, the colonial farmer had to expect an acre of land in 1980 to be worth $106,160 for him to be on the margin of indifference between conservation and extensive use. With a discount rate of 10 percent, he had to expect a 1980 value of $732,167 to justify conservation. Since fertile land on the eastern seaboard today is worth much less than this, not only was the individual farmer better off by mining the soil fertility, but society in general also received a higher value from the land resource.

The lesson for today is that extensive use of resources by no means implies waste. Whether we are wasting our valuable farmland depends upon the value of output produced from that land, the cost of other inputs, and the expected future value of the land. Private owners who are reducing soil fertility must believe that they are conserving on valuable labor and capital inputs. Those who convert agricultural land to urban uses must believe that future agricultural values will not warrant preservation. Before glibly accusing these farmers of waste, we must consider all of the economic variables.

Suggested Readings:

Johnson, Ronald N., and Gary D. Libecap, "Efficient Markets and Great Lakes Timber: A Conservation Issue Reexamined," *Explorations in Economic History*, 17 (October, 1980).

Scoville, Warren, "Did Colonial Farmers Waste Our Land?" *Southern Economic Journal*, XX (April, 1953).

VIII

Government and the Growth of the Economy

In the early days of the republic, government played a crucial role in creating a hospitable environment for economic activity. The Constitution provided for the enforcement of contracts under a system of law and order and was essential in protecting specific rights and obligations of private property. This kind of political stability in a society based on law is absolutely fundamental to the development of a market economy. But beyond these functions, how important was the government's active intervention in economic activity through public investment, tariffs, subsidies, land grants, and similar policies?[1] In other words, the state has both a protective and a productive role to play (see Chapter II). Up until now, we have concentrated on the protective role. We now turn to the government's productive function—that of providing public goods or of equating private and social rates of returns.

[1] This chapter is concerned with government subsidies and investment; it does not explore other ways by which government may affect the performance of the economy, such as public land policy (Chapter X) and monetary and fiscal policies (Chapter XIV).

GOVERNMENT INVOLVEMENT IN ECONOMIC ACTIVITY

Several studies have shown conclusively that government intervened significantly in the American economy during the nineteenth century.[2] In Massachusetts, government was involved in regulatory activities and in providing subsidies for economic activity. An even more striking case occured in Pennsylvania, where the government invested more than $100 million in public works and where, by 1844, there were public directors on the boards of more than 150 mixed (private and public) corporations. Studies have shown that state governments in the South were major underwriters of the railroad before the Civil War. Of $245 million invested in Southern railroads in 1860, more than 55 percent had been supplied through official public agencies. Between 1815 and 1860, states invested more than $136 million in canals— more than 73 percent of total investment. In Missouri, more than $23 million had been pledged to public improvement by 1860.

State government investments declined in the post–Civil War period. Local aid was considerable during this period, and many communities and counties spent substantial sums to encourage or to subsidize transport development, particularly railroads. The federal government outdid the states by providing 131 million acres in land grants to railroads for construction of transcontinental lines. This was in addition to the approximately 48 million acres that the railroads received from the states.

THE CONTRIBUTION OF GOVERNMENT INVESTMENT

We must be cautious when assessing the importance of government investments. It is one thing to point out the involvement of government at all levels in economic activity; it is another to attribute to it a significant share of the growth of the American economy. As yet, no work has been done that enables us to bridge this gap. Unfortunately, all too often the ideological attitudes of scholars toward government intervention have influenced their perspective on the past. What we need

[2] For examples, see Oscar Handlin and Mary Handlin, *Commonwealth: A Study of the Role of Government in the American Economy, Massachusetts, 1774–1861* (Cambridge, Mass.: Harvard University Press, 1969), and Louis Hartz, *Economic Policy and Democratic Thought: Pennsylvania, 1776–1869* (Cambridge, Mass.: Harvard University Press, 1948).

is an unbiased, systematic examination of the extent to which government activity did or did not promote economic growth. To date, there has been no such analysis.

Again, the hypothetical alternative is essential. We have to ask: What would have happened to the economy in the absence of government investment or promotion of a particular type of economic activity? During the nineteenth century, government's share of total reproducible wealth in the United States, like the realized income from government, was always a very small percentage of either total reproducible wealth or of national income. Crude estimates suggest that in each case it was not more than 5 percent of the total.

Therefore, if government did in fact play a significant, productive role in the economy, it must have been because its effects were larger than the quantitative data would indicate. To support this case, we must first have affirmative answers to the following theoretical issues:

1. Was the social rate of return on investments in certain areas higher than the private rate of return? That is, were certain kinds of economic activity more important and more profitable to society as a whole than they would have been to private business?[3]

2. Did the government deliberately invest in activities in which there was a significant difference between the private and social rate of return? Such differences may well have existed, but it is quite another matter to assert that the government was aware of the differences and judiciously made the right investments.

3. Was the magnitude of the social rate of return on government investment large enough to make an appreciable contribution to the economy's rate of growth?

First, there were clear differences between private and social rates of return in a number of economic activities. How important they were is hard to say. It is probably true that the capital market was imperfect in the early nineteenth century, and it would have been hard for private individuals or companies to amass sufficient capital to undertake some of the economic activities inaugurated by the state. This was particularly true regarding canals. It is widely held that, in underwriting canals, state governments made it possible to attract foreign capital.[4] There is evidence to suggest that this is, in fact, correct.

---

[3] Consider a simple illustration: A railroad that costs $100 million earns $10 million annually in net income. The private rate of return is 10 percent. Suppose that as a result of lower transportation costs, it also increases the income of the farmers along its route by $10 million annually. The social rate of return is 20 percent.

[4] It is important to realize that just because state government invested or made it possible to acquire capital from the London money market, government's contribution was not "indispensible." It simply means that otherwise the interest costs would have been higher or the project would have been delayed until it appeared more profitable to private investors.

It is also probable that in many transportation investments, returns to society were greater than they would have been to a private investor, who would have been limited in the amount of tolls or rates charged on a canal or a railroad. Therefore we may cautiously conclude that in some significant areas there were important differences between private and social rates of return in the economy in the nineteenth century.

Second, did the government realize these differences? That is, was the government a wise investor? New York State's investment in the Erie Canal immediately comes to mind. It was a brilliant venture that yielded handsome benefits to society. But we can also mention the Pennsylvania Main Line Canal, a rather spectacular and costly failure. When we assess the total investment in canals, the results are still inconclusive (see Table VIII.1). There were some, such as the Ohio canals, in which the substantial investments of the state may or may not have been successful and worthwhile for society. Others were clear failures and went bankrupt. The same pattern of success and failure typifies many of the other states' projects as well as the local under-writing of economic activity that took place in the nineteenth century. Consequently, it is not possible at this point to determine what the total outcome would be if the necessary research were done.

Third, even if answers to the first two questions had led us to conclude that government investment was a positive contribution, we would still have to know whether its magnitude was significant. For example, take 10 percent as the government's percentage of gross capital formation in the nineteenth century and assume that the social rate of return on *all* that investment was double the rate in the private sector. If the growth rate of the gross national product (GNP) was 4.5 percent per year, then the government's contribution would be 20 percent of the contribution of capital to the growth rate.

Clearly, however, capital *alone* does not account for the total *extensive* and *intensive* growth of the economy—which is what the 4.5 percent is measuring. That is, the 4.5 percent figure measures increased output as a result of increases both in *inputs* and in *efficiency* of productive factors. Population expansion of more than 80 million during the nineteenth century and the resultant increase in the labor force contribute an important part of the 4.5 percent. Economies of scale that are not included would be another important contributor. Therefore, if we say that the capital contributed two-thirds of this growth rate, then 20 percent of 3 percent is the government's contribution, or six-tenths of 1 percent per year. Even this figure assumes that none of the resources devoted to government investment would have been replaced by private investment if government intervention had been absent. If we assume more reasonably that half of this investment would have been profitable for the private sector, then government's contribution to the growth rate would have been an increase in output of three-tenths of 1 percent per year. This is certainly a significant figure, but it does not bear out statements that the roles of local, state, and national government were indispensable. Since we have deliberately used apparently overstated figures, the implication is that the necessary research will show that the *overall* contribution of government investment in the nineteenth century was modest.

There are reasons to believe that government activity will not always be optimal, either in amount or in the type of endeavors undertaken. Some individuals will find it to their advantage to attempt to capture the government's monopoly on coercion in order to secure control over resources without having to bid them from alternative uses. Others will find it useful to use their time and talent to prevent those coercive takings. Once government identifies and becomes involved in solving what may be very real social problems (public goods problems), there is always the chance of capture by special interest groups. Efforts to increase the probability of such capture or to prevent it can lead to wasted resources and retarded economic growth.

The possibility of such resource waste is strengthened by the incidence of cost and benefits of many government programs. These programs often favorably affect a small, identifiable, easily organized group in the economy. Members of the group find it to their advantage to argue in favor of government action. But the costs of this action are usually spread over the economy at large in the form of marginally higher taxes. Therefore, those paying for the program often do not find it advantageous to speak out against the government intervention. It may not even pay them to secure enough information to understand what the program is and how much it will cost.

THE PRODUCTIVE ROLE OF GOVERNMENT

Despite the problems in securing the correct type and amount of government activity, it appears that there have been several areas of intervention that demonstrate the productive role of government. Public education has received the most conspicuous state and local government contributions. The public school system has been an important stimulus to the growth of human capital in the United States. With the passage of the Morrill Act in 1862, the land grant college made possible a wider spread of higher education than would have occurred without it. Private education at all levels would have experienced greater expansion in the absence of public education, but it would have probably resulted in more unequal distribution of income than actually has prevailed. What, then, was the social rate of return on education in nineteenth-century America? Little research has been done, but our impression of the importance of human capital and economic development suggests that it was important and worthy of far more attention than it has received.

Is it possible to measure government's contribution to the growth of output in a specific sector of the economy? The answer is clearly "yes." But instead of the impressionistic accounts that have characterized past studies, we must use systematic economic analysis and empirical data to achieve useful results. Consider the case of government research in agriculture.[5]

A study by John Kendrick shows that productivity in agriculture increased very little between 1900 and 1920, but thereafter it rose very rapidly.[6] Ever since 1887, with the passage of the Hatch Act, the federal government and numerous state agencies have expended substantial sums of money in agricultural research.[7] Because of the difficulty of defining and enforcing property rights in new knowledge, the government clearly had a productive role to play in subsidizing such research. What has been the contribution of this research to the observed productivity increase? What is the social rate of return on this investment by the government? In *Economic Organization of Agriculture*,[8] Theodore Schultz presents systematic evidence that shows a high rate of return on investments in research by agencies of the United States Department of Agriculture as well as by state experiment stations. He finds the overall return on research in agriculture to be approximately 30 percent.

The spectacularly successful case of hybrid corn reveals an even higher social rate of return.[9] Hybrid corn yields are 15 to 20 percent higher than those of the earlier open-pollinated varieties. Using the hypothetical alternative, we can measure what the value of output would have been in the absence of hybrid corn against the value of output that actually existed as a result of its development. Against

---

[5] For a summary of agricultural research productivity, see Vernon W. Ruttan, "Bureaucratic Productivity: The Case of Agricultural Research," *Public Choice* 35 (1980), pp. 529–547.

[6] *Productivity Trends in the United States* (Princeton, N.J.: Princeton University, 1961).

[7] An intriguing question is raised by the failure of productivity to expand substantially until more than 30 years after the beginning of this research.

[8] New York: McGraw-Hill, 1953, Chapter VII.

[9] The following section comes from Zvi Griliches, "Research Costs and Social Returns—Hybrid Corn and Related Innovations," *JPE*, LXVI, No. 5 (October, 1958).

Table VIII.1 Government Investments in Canals

State	Canal	Cost ($000)
	I. *Probably successful:*	
N.Y.	Erie Canal	$ 7,143
N.Y.	Champlain Canal	921
N.Y.	Oswego Canal	2,512
Ohio	Ohio Canal	4,245
Pa.	Delaware Division Canal	1,543
	TOTAL SUCCESSFUL CANALS	$ 16,364
	II. *Probably not successful:*	
Ohio	Miami and Erie Canal	5,920
Ohio	Wahlhonding Canal	607
Ohio	Hocking Canal	975
Ohio	Wabash and Erie Canal	500
N.Y.	Black River Canal	3,157
N.Y.	Genesea Valley Canal	5,663
N.Y.	Chenango Canal	2,316
Pa.	Mainline Canal[a]	16,473
Pa.	5 Penn. Lateral Canals[b]	15,033
Ind.	Wabash Canal	6,325
Ind.	Whitewater Canal	1,400
Ill.	Illinois and Michigan	6,558
Md.	Chesapeake and Ohio[c]	11,071
Va.	James and Kanawhas[d]	10,436
	Total unsuccessful canals	$ 86,434
	TOTAL CANAL INVESTMENT	$102,798

[a] Mainline Canal cost includes railroad connections.
[b] The five canals were: the Susquehanna Division Canal, the French Creek Canal, Beaver Canal, the North Branch Division Canal, and the West Branch Division Canal.
[c] Private company whose stock was largely owned by Maryland, Virginia, and the United States government.
[d] The $5.5 million of stock was purchased by Virginia, Richmond, and Lynchburg.

Source: Roger Ransom, "Canals and Development: A Discussion of the Issues," *AER*, LIV, No. 2 (May, 1964), 375.

this value, we must charge the total costs of research and development as well as any additional costs involved in using hybrid corn seed versus the open-pollinated varieties (see Table VIII.2).[10] As of 1955, for a research expenditure of $3 million, the net social returns were $248 million; that is, the social rate of return on this investment was at least 700 percent.

[10] We are omitting from this discussion a large number of technical issues in economics, such as the problems of present worth, the appropriate interest rate, and the assumed supply and demand elasticity.

Public health was another area that had strong public goods characteristics. If infectious diseases were reduced, it was difficult to exclude those who had benefited but had not paid for the reduction. Therefore, private producers, dependent only on voluntary purchase of their product, would significantly underproduce the commodity in question. In this case, the coercive power of government was very useful in solving the free rider problem.

Edward Meeker estimated the social rate of return on investment in public health from 1880 to 1910, when there were dramatic improvements in the health of city dwellers.[11] For instance, the life ex-

Table VIII.2   Hybrid Corn: Estimated Research Expenditures and Net Social Returns, 1910–1955 (millions of 1955 dollars)

Year	Total research expenditures (private and public)	Year	Total research expenditures (private and public)	Net social returns[a]
1910	0.008	1933	0.584	0.3
1911	0.011	1934	0.564	1.1
1912	0.010	1935	0.593	2.9
1913	0.016	1936	0.661	8.3
1914	0.022	1937	0.664	21.2
1915	0.032	1938	0.721	39.9
1916	0.039	1939	0.846	60.3
1917	0.039	1940	1.090	81.7
1918	0.039	1941	1.100	105.3
1919	0.044	1942	1.070	124.3
1920	0.052	1943	1.390	140.4
1921	0.068	1944	1.590	158.7
1922	0.092	1945	1.600	172.6
1923	0.105	1946	1.820	184.7
1924	0.124	1947	1.660	194.3
1925	0.139	1948	1.660	203.7
1926	0.149	1949	1.840	209.8
1927	0.185	1950	2.060	209.0
1928	0.210	1951	2.110	218.7
1929	0.285	1952	2.180	226.7
1930	0.325	1953	2.030	232.1
1931	0.395	1954	2.270	234.2
1932	0.495	1955	2.790	239.1
		Annually after 1955	3.000	248.0

[a] Net of seed production cost but not net of research expenditures. Net social returns are zero before 1933.

[11] "The Social Rate of Return on Investment in Public Health, 1880–1910," *JEH*, XXXIV, No. 2 (June, 1974).

pectancy of newborn males in New York City rose from 29 years in 1880 to 45 years in 1910. This improvement was largely attributable to the decline of infectious disease, which in turn was strongly correlated with the installation of sanitary sewers and the provision of essential supplies of pure drinking water. Meeker did not try to measure all of the benefits from the improved health of city residents, but he did estimate the returns to two components: (1) the dollar value in the reduction of work time lost because of the reduced incidence of certain diseases and (2) the dollar value of increased life expectancy. When comparing these benefits with the costs of the sewer and water systems, he found a social rate of return of between 6 and 16 percent. This was considerably above the private rate of return for most investments during the period, and Meeker concluded that the investment in public health was economically sound.

The methods used here are similar to those of "benefit-cost analysis" that have been developed to measure the rate of return upon government investments, particularly in the field of water resources. It is clear that some kinds of returns are extremely difficult to quantify. Nevertheless, the development of this systematic method for measuring the rate of return upon government investment today points the way toward the kinds of research that are necessary to evaluate the contributions of government of yesterday.

IX

Ships, Railroads, and Economic Growth

Improvements in transportation during the nineteenth century have explained a substantial part of the development of the American economy. Most economic historians have seen steam power for land and water transportation as the essence of the Industrial Revolution extending to transportation. In light of the importance attributed to industrialization in the growth process, it is not surprising that the steamship and the railroad were deemed indispensable to the expansion of international trade and to promoting the settlement and economic development of a continent.

In addition to its revolutionary role in lowering transportation costs, the railroad has also been credited with having additional substantial effects on economic development. The amount of capital invested in railroads in the nineteenth century made it the first billion dollar industry in the United States by the time of the Civil War. It was a large-scale industry and used in the course of its construction iron, steel, machinery, and timber, thereby promoting expansion in still other industries. Finally, the railroad required the development of sophisticated methods of large-scale business organization and has been considered a pioneer in the development of corporate organization in the United States.

Impressions, however, are no substitute for a systematic analysis that suggests a different interpretation of the role that transportation played in the nineteenth-century economy. To put this role in perspective, let us examine the costs of transportation, the investment induced by transportation enterprises, the organizational improvements effected by large-scale transportation media, and the relocation of economic activity as a result of changing transportation costs.

THE CHANGING COSTS OF TRANSPORTATION

Figure IX.1 gives us some notion of how ocean transportation costs fell from the early nineteenth to the early twentieth century. The black line is an index of freight rates themselves over this period; the white line shows the freight rate index divided by a price index for the period, so that we can see how the freight rates fell relative to the general

Figure IX.1   INDEX OF U.S. EXPORT FREIGHT RATES, 1814–1913

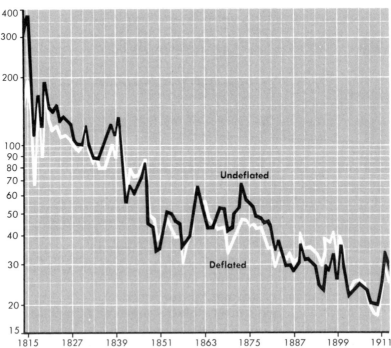

Source: Douglass C. North, "The Role of Transportation in the Economic Development of North America," paper presented to The International Congress of the Historical Sciences (Vienna, August 1965) and published in *Les grandes voies maritimes dans le monde XVe–XIXe siècles* (Paris, 1965).

price level. The chart shows that the most striking fall of ocean freight rates occurred between 1815 and 1850, followed by a period in which freight rates fell very little. Then they fell somewhat more modestly in the years between 1863 and 1908.

Although the steamship accommodated most passenger travel as early as 1850, the sailing ship continued to carry the majority of bulk goods until much later. Indeed, as late as 1880 most goods carried in ocean transportation were going by sail, and the changeover to steam did not occur in most of the long-haul routes until the end of the nineteenth century, when the triple-expansion engine made steam competitive. Some routes, such as the 14,000-mile long haul of grain from the Pacific Northwest to Liverpool, were still dominated by sailing ships until World War I. In short, it took the steamship approximately eighty years from its inception at the beginning of the nineteenth century to replace the sailing ship in the carriage of most bulk commodities. Yet the decline in transportation rates was most rapid during a period when the sail dominated ocean shipping. Even after 1870, improvement in the efficiency of sailing ships enabled the sailing vessel to compete with the steamship until the end of the century. Clearly, the sailing ship and not the steamship was mainly responsible for the dramatic fall in ocean transportation costs during the nineteenth century.

There was a decline in inland freight rates from 1784 to 1900. Since the rates shown in Figure IX.2 are not adjusted for differences in the price level, some of the movement reflects changes in general prices rather than real changes in transportation costs. The pattern of rate change is so great, however, that such a bias does not alter the picture very much. The major decline in inland transportation rates is a result of the difference between wagon and water rates. Note that the upstream and downstream river rates and canal rates are consistently lower than railroad rates. The dramatic technological change in inland transportation was not the result of the railroad (which we customarily think of) but rather the extensive use of inland waters. The consequent decline in rates for upstream river transportation after 1816 directly reflects the use of steamboats on the Mississippi River and its tributaries. James Mak and Gary Walton have found that the productivity of these steamboats on Western rivers increased between 4 and 6 percent annually from 1815 to 1860.[1] They estimate that in downstream transportation, even flatboat productivity increased by 2 percent annually prior to the Civil War.

---

[1] James Mak and Gary Walton, "Steamboats and the Great Productivity Surge in River Transportation" *JEH* (September, 1972), pp. 619–40.

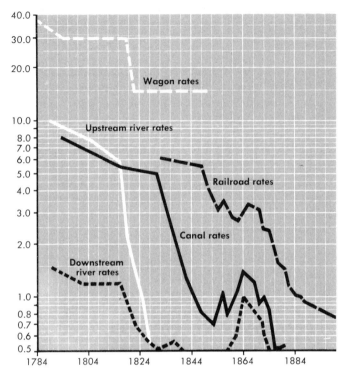

Source: North, "The Role of Transportation in the Economic Development of North America."

Figure IX.2   GENERAL PATTERN OF INLAND FREIGHT RATES, 1784–1900

Railroad rates fell dramatically throughout the century, but they remained higher than water rates. The railroad's domination of inland transportation during the last half of the nineteenth century, therefore, must have been due to reasons other than the direct one of simply offering lower ton-mile rates. This subject will be examined further at the end of the chapter.

INVESTMENT INDUCED BY TRANSPORTATION ENTERPRISES

The expansion of the railroad into every corner of the United States was certainly dramatic in the nineteenth century (see Figure IX.3). Increased railroad mileage suggests the way in which the railroad came to dominate internal transportation and the investment that was necessary to build such an immense system (see Table IX.1). Induced investment in other industries, however, does not necessarily benefit the economy, since improved productivity has already been passed on to the consumer in the form of lower transportation rates. Investments in other enterprises—iron, steel, timber, machinery, and so forth—increase productivity only to the extent that they make possible lower

Figure IX.3   EXPANSION OF RAILROAD MILEAGE, 1838–1899

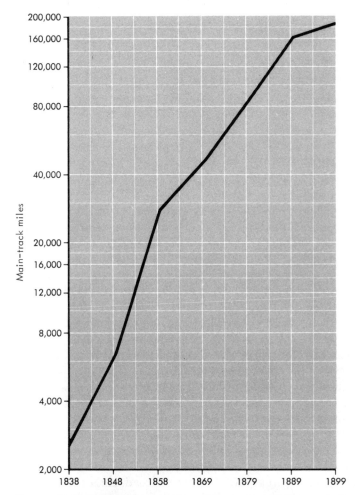

Source: Albert Fishlow,"Productivity and Technological Change in the Railroad Sector, 1840–1910," *Output, Employment, and Productivity in the United States after 1800* (New York: National Bureau of Economic Research, 1966), p.596.

Table IX.1 Real Net Capital Stock in Railroads, 1838–1909 (in millions of 1909 dollars)

End of Year	Equipment	Track	Total[a]
1838	$ 2.9	$ 79.8	$ 82.7
1848	11.4	219.4	230.9
1858	59.2	1,000.1	1,059.2
1869	111.7	1,629.4	1,741.1
1879	286.1	3,011.2	3,297.4
1889	606.8	5,867.2	6,474.0
1899	749.6	6,811.0	7,560.6
1909	1,658.2	8,799.7	10,457.9

[a] Totals adjusted to nearest thousand.

Source: Fishlow, "Productivity and Technological Change in the Railroad Sector, 1840–1910," p. 606.

costs in those industries, costs that would not have been reduced without the railroad's demand.

THE WAY TO RUN A RAILROAD—OR A FACTORY

The railroad was clearly the first large-scale enterprise in America, the kind of enterprise that required a corporate form of organization and the solution of complex management problems. It is difficult to assess the importance of the railroad's role in this process. One is tempted to believe that the railroad was a dependent variable; that is, given the gradual development of large-scale enterprise, a learning process was inevitable whatever the industry was. Since manufacturing was also developing large-scale organization by the end of the nineteenth century, such improvement in efficiency might have been the result of expansion in the size of the manufacturing firm.

The institutions for developing and financing the railroad paved the way for general improvements in organization, but they were not an unmitigated gain. Some aspects of railroad financing and organization in the United States were clearly detrimental. We have all heard of the financial manipulations of railroad financiers from the 1870s to 1900—manipulations that led to substantial watering of stock, that is, to expansion in the amount of nominal capital without really increasing the tangible earning power of the railroad. As a result, railroad financiers entered into a series of titanic battles in which bondholders—often British bondholders—frequently suffered at the expense of the manipulators. The famous episode of Drew, Fisk, and

Gould and the Erie Railroad was not an isolated case. Wild railroad-financing schemes persisted until the end of the century. Clearly, these schemes had involved some costs to improving organization, in that they had made risks higher. American and English investors were more reluctant to invest in railroads than they would have been had management been more responsible. Railroad finance, therefore, was sometimes a detriment to better economic organization and to improvements in the capital market. The actual costs have never been ascertained, but they were doubtless of some significance. Moreover, they afford a counterweight to whatever importance the railroad had as an agent in improving our knowledge about large-scale business organization.

RELOCATION OF ECONOMIC ACTIVITY

There is little evidence that the falling costs of transportation, particularly ocean transportation, led to the relocation of major forms of economic activity in the United States. Perhaps the greatest impact was on other countries. For example, the dramatic fall in the costs of inland and ocean transportation carrying grain and other foodstuffs to Europe hastened the relative decline of European agricultural production. The development of the North Pacific grain trade from Seattle and Portland to Liverpool was a case in point. A major new wheat-producing area was brought into the world market by two factors: first, a decline in the inland transportation costs of shipping wheat from the inland empire to Seattle and Portland; and second, the savings effected by a more efficient ocean transportatioon around Cape Horn. This is, however, probably the most dramatic case in which costs of transportation by sea affected the development of a new economic activity in the United States.

To what extent was economic activity internally relocated by the railroad? It is apparent that relative to other regions, manufacturing declined substantially in New England and slightly in the Middle Atlantic states from 1859 to 1914 while it increased in other areas (see Table IX.2). Activity in the Southeast declined until 1879 and then grew substantially. In the far West, activity increased at a much later period, and the Plains states grew slightly. How much of this changing pattern was due to the railroads? Some of it surely was. The shift of textiles from New England into the South was probably accounted for, at least in part, by the growth of railroad transportation in the South after 1889. Some industries were resource oriented, and the railroad

Table IX.2 Regional Employment in Manufacturing (percent of total U.S. mfg. employees)

	1859	1869	1879	1889	1899	1904	1909	1914
New England	29.88	26.76	24.31	20.57	18.91	17.87	17.30	16.83
Mid. Atlantic	41.66	39.52	42.04	38.69	37.54	36.99	35.82	35.89
Great Lakes	12.09	18.36	19.19	22.29	22.65	22.29	22.73	23.73
Southeast	9.80	8.48	7.57	8.90	11.55	12.87	13.61	13.05
Plains	2.30	4.79	4.46	6.01	5.41	5.37	5.32	5.10
Southwest	0.34	0.37	0.44	0.67	0.79	0.97	1.26	1.30
Mountain	0.03	0.17	0.31	0.49	0.71	0.69	0.82	0.82
Far West	3.90[a]	1.54	1.70	2.37	2.43	2.93	3.14	3.26

[a] Including gold mining.

Source: Figures for 1859 are from U.S. Census Office, *The Eighth Census: Manufacturers of the United States in 1860* (Washington: GPO, 1865). These are the raw "number of hands employed" figures and are not strictly comparable with those of subsequent years.

From 1869 to 1909 inclusive, figures are from Richard A. Easterlin, "Estimates of Manufacturing Activity," *Population Redistribution and Economic Growth, United States, 1870–1950* (Philadelphia: The American Philosophical Society, 1957), I, 684. These figures have been adjusted from original census data in several ways and are rounded to the nearest hundreds.

Figures for 1914 are based on the "average wage earners" category of U.S. Census Office, *Abstract of the Census of Manufacturers, 1914* (Washington: GPO 1917). In order to make them roughly comparable to the 1869–1909 data, percentage changes from 1909 to 1914 in the census figures were calculated, and these were applied to the 1909 figures from the above source. This assumes that structural changes in employment were not great between 1909 and 1914.

made it possible for plants to be nearer their natural resources. The usefulness of timberland and other natural resources was certainly increased as the railroad developed. On the other hand, the railroad could take credit for the modification, rather than the initiation, of industrial activities in certain areas, particularly in the Middle Atlantic and Great Lakes states. Transportation needs in these areas were already met by water, and at most the railroad led to rather minor relocations of industrial activity.

It is clear that the acceleration of settlement and agricultural production in the western two-thirds of the United States was strikingly influenced by the railroads. The wheat industry shifted westward into the Great Plains, and new agricultural areas opened up where transportation was available. Even there, however, the railroad's significance can be overstated. Robert Fogel has estimated that although less than half the land mass of the United States in 1890 was within forty miles of a navigable waterway (the limits of feasible commercial agriculture), more than three-quarters of the agricultural land was within such limits.[2] The great bulk of the land outside of these limits

[2] Robert William Fogel, *Railroads in American Economic Growth* (Baltimore: Johns Hopkins University Press, 1964), pp. 80–81.

was between the 100th meridian and the Sierra Nevada mountains; and as of 1890, it produced only 2 percent of the country's agricultural products.

WERE RAILROADS "ESSENTIAL" TO GROWTH?

Two studies have helped to fuel the controversy over how much influence the railroad had on American economic growth. In 1964, Robert Fogel wrote *Railroads in American Economic Growth*,[3] in which he estimated that in 1890 the social savings of the railroad was approximately 5 percent of the gross national product. Fogel's conclusion was based on the volume of goods moved by the railroad in 1890. He estimated the cost of moving that same volume by the next best alternative, primarily water transportation, and adjusted his conclusion for differential cargo losses and inventory costs.[4] This finding was perhaps the most controversial result of the new economic history, since it differed widely from the general impression of the railroad's indispensability. In 1965, *American Railroads and the Transformation of the Ante-Bellum Economy*, by Albert Fishlow, was published.[5] Fishlow showed that there was a social savings of 5 percent in 1860, and any reasonable extrapolation of that figure to 1890 would lead to a figure in excess of 10 percent. The difference between the two figures stemmed not only from measuring different things (Fogel used an estimate of the costs of transporting agricultural goods) but also from a basic difference over what the costs would have been in moving the goods by the next best alternative.

The controversy has been discussed endlessly in the journals.[6] At stake is a basic dilemma surrounding the use of the hypothetical alternative or counterfactual proposition. The construction of a hypothetical alternative in this case means building a model of how the economy would have performed under different circumstances—that is, without railroads. This alternative, in effect, must be a general equilibrium model that would allow for the total consequences to the

---

[3] *Ibid.*

[4] Fogel slights the issue that some goods (perishables, for example) could not have moved at all by alternatives, and so he added inventory costs to understate the difference. Also, he does not include passenger savings, which were substantial. See J.H. Boyd and Gary Walton, "The Social Savings from Nineteenth Century Rail Passenger Services," *EEH*, IX (Spring, 1972).

[5] Cambridge, Mass.: Harvard University Press.

[6] See citations in bibliography to Chapter IX. Detailed criticisms concerned whether rates measured social savings appropriately as well as exactly what is meant by social savings.

economy if the railroad were absent. Once we begin to consider the magnitude and ramifications of such an absence, it is easy to see what widely divergent results we could get. What would have happened to other transportation means, to technological change, and to all of the industries that supplied the railroads?

The hypothetical alternative is obviously essential to the study of economic history, but it will hardly resolve a controversy that involves repercussive effects of the magnitude possible here. In considering the railroad, we are dealing with the major single source of investment during much of the late nineteenth century and trying to ascertain all of its consequences for sixty years. That burdens the hypothetical alternative with too many possible and reasonable alternative developments. We do not mean to suggest that Fogel and Fishlow have not written valuable studies; to the contrary, the studies have not only contributed a great deal to our understanding of railroad history but have forced a clarification of the exact nature of what is meant by social savings and of the limitation inherent in the use of the counterfactual proposition.

X

Land Policy and the Westward Movement

Perhaps the most dramaic event in American economic history is the settling of our continental territory. When the Declaration of Independence was enacted, only the eastern seaboard had been settled by the British, although some hardy souls had crossed the mountains and established themselves on the other side of the Appalachian Mountains in the Ohio Valley. Farther west, the country was largely unknown to white men. A vast land area was settled after 1776, and by the 1890s the superintendent of the United States Census had reported that the frontier had disappeared.

Over the years, the United States acquired land in big chunks: the Louisiana Purchase in 1803; Florida in 1819; and Texas, California, and the territory of Oregon in the 1840s. By 1853, with the Gadsden Purchase of a strip of land on the Mexican border, the contiguous territorial boundaries of the continental United States were established.

Settling these areas was a much longer and more dramatic story. The Lewis and Clark expedition followed the Missouri River to its headwaters, crossed the Rocky Mountains, and spent a winter at the mouth of the Columbia River. When they returned, the explorers told a story of an extraordinary land full of promise—a land that was to dominate much of our history, as venturesome Americans looked over the new frontier and settled it. Fur traders came hard on the heels of Lewis and Clark. In fact, some members of the expedition went back upriver to search for beaver pelts. Then came the farmer and the miner, and cities developed as the frontier receded. The center of population continued to move west during the nineteenth century as this expanse of territory was settled and developed.

PUBLIC LAND POLICY

The exciting story of geographical expansion has long preoccupied and inspired Americans. It has also presented extraordinary economic problems. Beginning in the 1780s, the federal government was permitted to gain title to land west of the Appalachians—land originally claimed by the individual states. From an institutional perspective, an important decision made early in our history was that these lands would not be retained by the government but would be transferred to private ownership. Such ownership was necessary if net private and social returns were to be equated, thus promoting productivity and growth.

This point decided, the government had several different and sometimes contradictory objectives that could be reached by the sale of public lands. The prime objective was to aid in the settlement of the United States and to create conditions that would favor economic development. At the same time the government wanted to raise revenues; and public land sales proved to be a major, although irregular, source of revenue for a long period in our history.

There were many possible methods for making these lands available to the government. Since each method seemed to have a different distribution of benefits and costs, disposal of the public domain has become one of the most controversial subjects in American history. Table X.1 shows how public land disposal changed between 1785 and 1916 as a result of changes in federal legislation.

In 1785, the first public land disposal legislation was passed. It not only set minimum acreage to be sold and its price, but it also laid out the township system of land division that has characterized American surveying ever since. Less durable have been the minimum standards, which shifted drastically from 640 acres or more in 1785 to 40 acres in 1832 and back to 640 acres by 1916. In the meantime, the minimum price per acre started at $1.00 in 1785, went to $2.00 until 1804, and dropped to $1.25 between 1820 and 1832, and eventually to nothing (free). The terms, cash or credit, varied. Prior to 1862 the general system of distribution was to put the lands up for auction. If no one bid above the set minimum, the land was not sold. After 1862 distribution was based mainly on development of the land.

Since the Revolutionary War, the government has given away substantial tracts of land. War veterans, for example, received military bounty warrants entitling them to land. As large numbers of these warrants accumulated, they were traded actively and were bought and sold like any other valuable claim. As noted in previous chapters, both the federal government and the states gave public lands to the railroads to encourage the building of transcontinental systems. A total of 180 million acres went toward this objective, with the Northern Pacific Railroad receiving the lion's share but other lines also benefiting.

By the middle of the nineteenth century, "giving away" land basically replaced land sales. In 1841, the Preemption Act was enacted to protect squatters—those eager settlers who went ahead of the surveyers and, holding no title to their land, were faced with eviction, sometimes by government troops. The Preemption Act gave squatters first rights to purchase their land if they had settled on it before the survey. In 1854, the Graduation Act was passed, and lands that had not sold at the government minimum could now be sold at lower prices. Then came the landmark legislation that has frequently been considered a watershed in the history of America's public lands—the Homestead Act of 1862. This act stipulated that a bona fide settler could receive title to 160 acres free and clear (320 acres if he were married), provided that he lived on the land or cultivated it for five years. It became clear, however, that additional legislation was needed, particularly in areas where mining and lumber industries were involved. This led to the Timber Culture Act in 1873, the Desert Act of 1877, and the Timber Cutting Act and Timber and Stone Act of 1878.

After the passage of these acts, less effort was made to put land into private ownership. Homesteading continued into the twentieth century, but the late nineteenth century witnessed the reservation of considerable amounts of Western land. The major goal was no longer to establish private rights in the land. Since the land reserved for public ownership was not very productive, vast tracts of marginal timber and grazing land became part of the public domain. As a result of this reservation, nearly one-third of the United States is now owned by the federal government, and in some states federal ownership runs as high as 95 percent.

ANALYSIS OF LAND POLICY: IMPACT ON GROWTH

The impact of public land policy on economic growth has been a controversial issue in American history. In general, historians have been extremely critical of land policy, believing that it rewarded greed and speculation. From these criticisms and accompanying debates, three

Table X.1 Major Public Land Laws, 1785–1916

Year	Price (per acre)	Size (acres)	Conditions
1785	$1 minimum	640 or more	Cash sale; amended in 1787 to provide for payment of one-third in cash, the remainder in three months.
1796	$2 minimum	640 or more	One-half of purchase price paid within thirty days the remainder within one year.
1800	$2 minimum	320 or more	One-fourth of purchase price paid within thirty days, then annual installments of one-fourth for three years, at 6 percent interest.
1804	$2 minimum ($1.64 for cash)	160 or more	Credit as in act of 1800; discount to $1.64 per acre for cash payment.
1820	$1.25 minimum	80 or more	End of credit system; cash payment only.
1830	$1.25 minimum	160 maximum	Squatters on public domain land allowed to purchase their tracts at the minimum price (preemption); temporary act, had to be renewed biennially.
1832	$1.25 minimum	40 or more; 160 limit on preemption	Cash purchase only; right of preemption reaffirmed.
1841	$1.25 minimum	40 or more; 160 limit on preemption	Cash purchase only; established right of preemption, doing away with necessity of renewing legislation.
1854 (Graduation Act)	12.5 cents minimum	40 or more	Reduction of the sale price of land in proportion to the length of time it had been on the market; price ranged from $1 for land unsold for 10 years to 12.5 cents for land unsold for thirty years.

Year (Act)	Price	Acreage	Provisions
1862 (Homestead Act)	zero	160 or less	Payment of an entry fee and five years' continuous residence; land could be preempted after six months' residence for $1.25 per acre cash.
1873 (Timber Culture Act)	zero	160	Cultivation of trees on one-quarter of a 160-acre plot gave the settler title to the entire 160 acres; amended in 1878 to require the cultivation of trees on only one-sixteenth of the plot.
1877 (Desert Land Act)	$1.25	640; reduced to 320 maximum in 1890	Sale of a section of land to a settler on condition that it be irrigated within three years; amended in 1891 to increase the amount of improvements required, with one-eighth of the land to be under cultivation; payment to be 25 cents at time of entry, $1 at the time of making proof of compliance with the law.
1878 (Timber and Stone Act)	$2.50	160 or less	Sale of lands chiefly valuable for timber or stone resources to bona fide settlers and mining interests.
1909 (Enlarged Homestead Act)	zero	320 acres	Five years' residence with continuous cultivation; designed for semi-arid lands that were nonirrigable and had no minerals or marketable timber.
1916 (Stock-Raising Homestead Act)	zero	640 acres	Designed for land useful only for grazing; conditions similar to those of previous Homestead laws.

Source: Lance E. Davis, Richard A. Easterlin, William N. Parker, et al., *American Economic Growth: An Economist's History of the United States* (New York: Harper & Row, 1972), pp. 104–105

basic questions emerge regarding land policy: First, how did land policy influence the rate of economic growth? Second, what was the impact of land speculation? Third, what impact did land policy have on income and wealth distribution?

While these questions have not been answered completely, the issues of public land policy can be sorted out by understanding the concept of economic rent.[1] In its simplest form, the term *economic rent* refers to the difference between the market value of output produced from a particular source and the cost of other inputs used to generate the output. In the case of land used in the production of wheat, for example, the value or rent of the land will move up and down as the value of the wheat and the costs of inputs change. It is reasonable to expect that for very low values of output or high production costs, the net value of production at a particular point in time could actually be negative.

Three factors greatly influenced land rents in the United States: (1) the rising value of outputs produced from the resource base; (2) declining transportation costs; and (3) technological change that reduced production costs. Population growth and the expansion of the market generated increases in the demand for agricultural outputs. The demand was not only from the growing East but from foreigners as well. Wheat, for example, became prominent as an export as a result of the Irish Famine in the 1840s and gained momentum after the Civil War. In addition, freight rates declined as the result of canals and waterways in the eastern half of the United States and of railroads in the western half (see Chapter IX). Finally, developments like the steel plow, the reaper, and the cotton gin along with new varieties of crops pushed the frontier westward.

These developments affected the time path of land rents and were reflected in land price movements. People surged into new lands from 1816 to 1818, in the 1830s, the 1850s, the late 1860s, and in the 1880s. Each surge was induced by a rapidly expanding demand that produced rising prices of agricultural goods. It is good to keep this in mind, because the decisiveness of such market influences is not included in many descriptions of westward settlement. The view that the West not only dominated our history but that it was a refuge in bad times for the poor and unemployed is simply untenable. In general, the unem-

---

[1] For two important articles addressing land policy and the concept of economic rent, see Taylor R. Dennen, "Some Efficiency Effects of Nineteenth-Century Federal Land Policy: A Dynamic Analysis," *Agricultural History* (October, 1977), pp. 718–36, and Gary D. Libecap and Ronald N. Johnson, "Property Rights, Nineteenth-Century Federal Timber Policy, and the Conservation Movement," *JEH* (March, 1979), pp. 129–42.

ployed and the poor did not have the means to go west and start farming. Indeed, most people moved west during good times, in periods of rising prices and expanding demand, when the prospects for making money from the new land looked brightest. These are the conditions that characterized the whole pattern of settlement.

Evidence suggests that when considering frontier America, we can expect a time path of rents from land in production to be like that depicted in Figure X.1. The suggestion is that at some early date, rents were negative, but over time conditions changed so that rents rose and eventually became positive. The important implication for land policy and economic growth is that there is an optimal time for bringing land into production. The net value of bringing a particular piece of land into production will be equal to the discounted annual rents over the production period. It is clear that the net present value of annual rents will be maximized if land is put into production at the point t^*. If land is brought into production prior to t^*, the negative rents for the early period must be subtracted from the positive rents that follow t^*. On the other hand, if land is brought into production after t^*, some positive rents will not be captured.

Using this analysis, there is good reason to expect that public land policy retarded growth by promoting production before t^*. Consider how property rights were assigned in many of the early land acts that provided for the outright sale of public lands. Under competitive bidding conditions, such allocation schemes would have encouraged

Figure X.1 PATH OF LAND RENTS OVER TIME

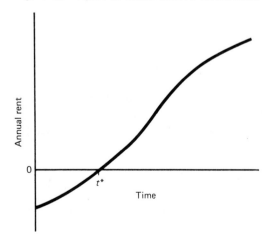

individuals to bid an amount equal to the net present value of the positive rents. Title to the land was exchanged for title to other assets in the form of money. Once title was established, the land would be brought into production at the socially and privately optimal time. Even if the land were sold before t^*, no production would occur until t^*. Under these conditions, land policy would have maximized economic growth by providing the necessary incentive structure and by encouraging production to begin at the optimal time.

The problem with land policy occurred when it encouraged people to settle on and produce from the land before t^*. Why would people settle when annual rents were negative? The answer is that they would do so if "early" settlement and production were the least costly (private cost) or only way to obtain title. For example, under the sales schemes, a minimum price per acre was set ranging from $1.00 to $2.00, a price that often exceeded the net present value of the land. A minimum price can be justified to cover the costs of surveying and registering titles, but these costs were probably less than a penny per acre. Since obtaining title through purchase required a payment in excess of the expected value, it is not surprising that individuals resorted to squatting on the land. In this way, they could obtain title on a "first come, first served" basis. In order to be first, people were willing to settle prematurely so that they could be certain to capture the positive rents of later years. Requirements of the homestead acts encouraged the same thing. In addition, settlers were required to produce from inefficiently sized parcels, to plow and cultivate areas better suited for grazing, and to irrigate land better left dry. Competition among squatters and homesteaders not only meant that they were willing to settle the land when the annual rents were negative, but in the limit, competition to get to the land first would result in settlement when the discounted value of rents became positive rather than when they were maximized. Therefore, squatting and homesteading lowered the growth rate by encouraging the waste of resources in the process of assigning private property rights to individuals. Through subsequent private sales of land, the country eventually arrived at a set of property rights that were more or less efficient; unfortunately, we got them through an inefficient process.

All systems of transferring ownership, of course, required transaction costs, but some necessitated a greater degree of rent dissipation than others. In a study of rent dissipation under the Timber and Stone Act and the Preemption Act, Libecap and Johnson estimated that "expenditures attributable to federal restrictions and which involved real resources, agent payment, development costs, and miscellaneous expenditures," amounted to between 60 percent (Timber and Stone Act) and 80 percent (Preemption Act) of the total land value.[2] While there is no good estimate of the total amount of resources expended in this manner, 27 percent of the public domain disposed of by the federal government was patented under the Homestead Acts. This led Taylor Dennen to conclude that "there is no reason to believe that the impact of the federal land-disposition system on the national economy was insignificant."[3]

SPECULATION AND INCOME DISTRIBUTION

Repetition of the terms *speculator* and *land monopolist* in the writings on public land policy necessitates a precise examination of these terms. Just what is speculation? When you buy an asset with a resale or rental value, you are speculating. In buying an asset, you forego buying other assets that offer prospective income streams. You are guessing about the future value of the asset. In the context of the rents described in Figure X.1, speculation simply means that people have different expectations about the rental path. Optimists will believe that t^* is earlier and rents are larger and will be the first to purchase or settle the land. The speculator performs the important function of bearing risks in the market economy, of improving knowledge about available opportunities, and of giving future generations a voice today, thereby making the market work more perfectly. It is hard to imagine any way that one could dispose of public land without speculation.

It is not hard to imagine, however, why individuals are hostile to speculation. Speculation, like other entrepreneurial activities, leaves the successful speculator with increased wealth. Though efficiency may be improved and the wealth of society may be increased, the likelihood is that there will be a redistribution of income. Although there is not evidence that all speculators earned high rates of return or that the average rate of return was high, some did extremely well.[4] Speculators earning a high rate of return received the larger piece of

[2] Libecap and Johnson, *Ibid.*, p. 137.

[3] Dennen, *Ibid.*, p. 736.

[4] A careful study by Allen and Margaret Bogue, "Profits and the Frontier Land Speculator," *JEH*, XVII (March, 1957), shows a widely varied pattern in which some cases of relatively high rates of return were matched by other cases of low or negative returns, so the general pattern does not appear to be one in which speculator profits were extremely high. See also R.P. Swierenga, *Pioneers and Profits: Land Speculation on the Iowa Frontier* (Ames: Iowa State University, 1968).

a larger pie. It is this "destabilizing" nature of speculation to which most people object.[5]

The term *land monopolist* is simply a misuse of the term *monopolist*. There is no meaningful sense in which a monopoly of land existed at any time during the nineteenth century. In fact, availability is the one clearly evident characteristic of the opening up of the public domain. There were always large amounts of land available from a number of sources. People who wanted land of any quality could always get it from the government or from a host of private sellers. That large blocks of land were at times held by individuals is in no sense an indication of land monopoly, unless the holders actually owned a large enough percentage of all available land that they could influence its overall price—and this never happened in America.

One criticism leveled against "land speculators" and "land monopolists" is that they impaired western movement by keeping large tracts of land off the market to obtain a higher price. Since the purpose of speculation is to make money, we would predict that the speculators would bring the land into production at the optimal time; that is, they would rent it, lease it, or sell it at t^*. To the extent that speculators bought up great tracts of land prior to t^*, they would not have placed the land into production. Such action, however, promotes rather than retards economic growth, since it maximizes the rental value of the land.

How did public land policies affect the distribution of wealth? Did these policies, as many historians contend, favor the rich at the expense of the poor? Without further research, our conclusions in this area must be tentative. There was one kind of redistribution about which we can be more definitive. We can say that inherent in giving away the land instead of selling it, taxpayers (rich and poor alike) were losers because the government had to collect revenue from other sources.

There have been no significant studies of the land disposal system's impact on income distribution or among the general populace. Nor has there been any examination of land grants to railroads or homesteaders that disclosed their effects on income distribution. If we had this information, we could compare it with a hypothetical alternative, which would be a system based on policies proposed by land reformers throughout the nineteenth century and implicit in many of the criticisms advanced by historians. It is clear that there is still much work to be done.

---

[5] For a more detailed discussion of the destabilizing nature of growth, see Chapter XII.

A LESSON FROM HISTORY:

Should We Sell our Land to Foreigners?

During the 1970s, increasing amounts of foreign capital flowed into the United States to purchase land and other assets. By 1975, 4.9 million acres of U.S. land were owned by foreigners and 6.2 million acres were leased. Although this amounts to less than 0.5 percent of all private land, concern over foreign ownership of agricultural land, forests, coal resources, and other real estate has brought pressure for laws regulating foreign investment in this country. The slightest hint of real estate purchases by OPEC nations brings local, state, and even national opposition.

Such opposition, however, has not typified the U.S. response to foreign investment. In 1791 the Secretary of the Treasury, Alexander Hamilton, stressed that foreign investments, "instead of being viewed as rival, ought to be considered as a most valued auxiliary, conducing to put in motion a greater quantity of productive labor and a greater portion of useful enterprise, than could exist without it." With this attitude, the U.S. spent the first 150 years after independence as a net creditor. Capital was attracted for the construction of railroads, canals, and highways. Between 1850 and 1900 aggregate foreign indebtedness grew from $217 million to $2 billion. Such indebtedness continued from 1916 to 1961 with foreign direct investments generally constituting between 25 percent and 35 percent of total long-term investment.

Although a complete series on alien ownership of land is not available, it is clear that foreign real estate holdings increased throughout the nineteenth century, reaching a zenith around 1900. After the Revolutionary War, land offices sprang up all over Europe with their emphasis on the sale of smaller parcels to emigrants. But the major stimulus to alien land ownership in the United States was provided by transcontinental railroads and the opening of the American West. "As stated by the *Liverpool Journal*, Americans do not sit and wait for emigrants to come; they send agents to England 'to tell us what is going on and to show the better class of emigrants what opportunities America has provided for them in the West.'"* Foreigners invested in railroad lands, state bonds, mortgage companies, and cattle ranches, and these investments led Herbert Brayer to conclude that "the contribution of this foreign enterprise in the West was incalculable."†

This conclusion cannot be ignored. Market signals generated capital flows that increased the incomes of foreigners and contributed significantly to total capital formation and economic growth in the United States. Without this foreign investment we certainly would have been poorer. Today foreign contributions to the capital stock and productivity are no less important. Although foreign in-

---

* Oscar O. Winter, "Promoting the American West in England, 1865–1890," *Journal of Economic History* 16 (December, 1956), 506.

† Herbert O. Brayer, "The Influence of British Capital on the Western Range-Cattle Industry," *Journal of Economic History: The Tasks of Economic History*, Supplement IX, 1949, 55.

vestments give some control of assets to aliens, the positive aspects of these investments should be remembered when policy is formulated.

Suggested Reading:

Economic Research Service, U.S. Department of Agriculture, *Foreign Investment in U.S. Real Estate.* Washington: G.P.O., 1976.

XI

Economic Growth and Agrarian Discontent, 1865–1914

From 1865 to 1914, economic growth was rapid, with real per capita income increasing at 2 percent per year and real gross national product (GNP) growing at approximately 4 percent per year. Thus the period between the Civil War and World War I was one of sustained economic growth in both intensive and extensive terms. In fact, there is probably not another period of similar length in American economic history with growth rates that high.

During this time, the frontier as a distinct line of settlement disappeared. Agricultural settlement continued to spread across the West, and there was more specialization in production. Continued transportation improvements integrated farmers into a national and world market, while the mechanization of many production processes greatly increased output beyond subsistence.

Although the Civil War was not a major impetus to accelerated industrial growth, from 1865 to 1914 manufacturing expanded. The United States became the leading industrial nation in the world, with about one-third of the world's manufacturing capacity. The story of industrial expansion in America is one of technological innovations fully exploited by entrepreneurs who operated in a hospitable institutional environment and is not unlike that of the Industrial Revolution in England. New forms of organization were necessary to reduce transaction costs in carrying out industrial expansion; and entrepreneurs, such as Carnegie, Rockefeller, and Ford, were active forces in creating new ways of monitoring and organizing production. The results of the dynamic changes in technology and in organizations in American industry can be seen in Figure XI.1. In the sixty-year period from 1839 to 1899, there was a forty-fold increase in the real value added by manufacturing.

Figure XI.1   VALUE ADDED BY MANUFACTURE (1879 PRICES)

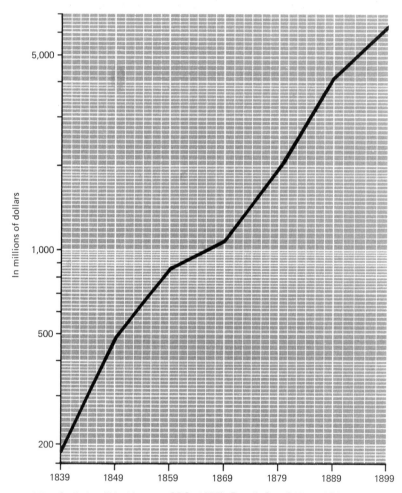

Source: *Hist. Statistics* (Washington: GPO, 1975), Part II, Ser. P10, p. 654.

THE SOURCES OF EXPANSION

What factors made this expansion possible? In agriculture, the existence of large amounts of land made increased output easily attainable (see Chapter X). Although this was not a period of sharply rising productivity in farming, rapid population growth in America did stimulate the demand for foodstuffs. In manufacturing, there are two distinct aspects of development: (1) the technological innovation that made possible the tremendous strides in industrial development and (2) special factors that made American manufacturing development increase at a greater rate than in the rest of the world.

There were revolutionary changes in almost every type of manufacturing during this period. Industrial innovations not only originated in the United States, but also in England, France, and Germany. The development of these innovations was accelerated by the rapid growth of scientific knowledge in the late nineteenth century and by the rising incomes and rapidly expanding demand that characterized the western world.

In one sense, there was a very real change in the manner in which technological progress occurred during this period. Prior to the middle of the nineteenth century, most technological events were largely independent of developments in basic science. But major scientific breakthroughs were required for most of the significant technological events after that date. In the earlier period, learning by doing was responsible for most of the technology developed, but only scientific experimentation can account for the later breakthroughs. Thus, the marriage of science and technology during the later part of the nineteenth century was a crucial development in our economic growth. The rise of the electrical industry was but one example of the results of formal training and scientific experimentation.

Nevertheless, it was the incentive structure that provided the hospitable environment for technological change. As markets expanded, there was undoubtedly a high social rate of return to new ideas. That property rights in ideas were reasonably well defined and enforced through trademarks, copyrights, trade secrets, and patent laws meant that inventors and innovators stood to capture a substantial share of the benefits created by their technological changes. Furthermore, the generally well-developed rights to property and income encouraged entrepreneurs to organize inputs, develop new forms of business structure, and generally search out ways of increasing productivity.

Two other aspects of industrial growth should be mentioned. First, America's labor supply was not purely indigenous but was augmented by a sizable immigration, especially in the last half of the nineteenth century. Between 1860 and 1920, the population of the United States tripled, with about 40 percent of that increase due to immigration. After 1900, the flow of immigrants became a flood, with more than 1 million new residents arriving annually in six of the fifteen years between 1900 and 1914. These newcomers were largely males in the productive ages, and they significantly increased the nation's human capital base.

The second factor in industrial growth was the development of the capital market. To understand this development, we need to know how savings were organized and channeled into the investments necessary to build factories and machinery, to clear and improve land, and to advance the working capital to maintain a labor force, inventories, and so forth.

Although the focus here is on the long-term capital market, it should be noted that between the Civil War and World War I the short-term market became more efficient. The banking system expanded enormously during that time, both in the number of banks and in the amount of loans in circulation. It was not until the end of the period that any semblance of central banking reemerged in America—a reemergence from the long era of dispute that followed the demise of the Second Bank of the United States, when President Andrew Jackson vetoed its rechartering in the 1830s. When the Federal Reserve System was created in 1914, a central banking system was reconstructed. But the story of banking and the money supply properly belongs in a study of economic fluctuations and variations in the rate of utilization of resources, and this will be explored later.

The major concern here is with the evolution of the long-term capital market—that is, the evolution of a system of financial intermediaries that managed to get savings to flow into the industries discussed in this chapter. The growth of investment banking in America can be traced back to the demand for large-scale financing for canals and railroads and to the development of a regular connection between English investors and American financial institutions. Gradually, some of the investment banks, having started as branches of English firms, developed into American houses and became the organizers of large-scale financing of major industries. Savings were held in trust, and savings banks, insurance companies, other repositories, and the investment banker formed "syndicates" to underwrite the bond issues that went to build railroads, steel mills, agricultural machinery factories, and other major projects. The growth of these savings institutions and financial intermediaries led to the increasing efficiency of the long-term capital market.

AGRARIAN DISCONTENT

With substantial economic growth resulting in rising per capita incomes throughout the period, one might suppose that most people were satisfied with the way the system was working. But this was not the case. Between the end of the Civil War and 1900, the agrarian sector of the economy was in a continuous state of turmoil and political unrest. A series of protest organizations and political parties evolved with the goal of improving the lot of the farmer, beginning in 1867 with the Granger Movement, and followed by the Greenback Movement, the Farmers' Alliances, and the Populist Party. These organizations were aimed at promoting a variety of economic policies, including railroad regulation, the formation of cooperatives, increased circulation of paper money as a means of raising the price level, and the demand for free coinage of silver and gold. The farmer was attempting to initiate fundamental reforms in the American economy. While the movements varied in intensity over time and among agricultural regions, they mirrored the farmers' widespread dissatisfaction. From the farmers' viewpoint, economic issues were central to the problems they faced. But was their perception consistent with the facts?

The major complaints of farmers were as follows: First, the prices of agricultural goods had fallen more than the prices of other goods, and they had done so because other prices had been held up by monopolistic elements in the economy. The purchasing power of the farmer, therefore, was falling. For every bushel of wheat sold, the farmer was able to buy less of the things he demanded. Second, railroad tycoons, grain elevator operators, and middlemen in general were using monopolistic practices to absorb the profits from agriculture, rather than passing on to the farmer the gains accruing from improved transportation and organization of the market. Third, the money lenders were robbing the farmer. The farmer felt that the eastern capitalist and his western equivalent in mortgage companies were deliberately using monopolistic practices, charging high rates to farmers, and imposing a particularly heavy burden during a period of expansion when most farmers needed such loans. Moreover, having to pay back a fixed debt was an even heavier burden in a period of falling prices, because the dollars paid toward the loan were worth more at the time of repayment than they had been when the debt was contracted.

Let us examine each complaint in turn. First, a comparison of the prices of farm commodities with those of all commodities in the War-ren–Pearson index fails to support the farmers' position on relative prices (see Figure XI.2 for the ratio of farm prices to all prices, or the agricultural terms of trade). Although there are real limitations in using the Warren–Pearson index, since it measures prices in New York, Cincinnati, and Chicago rather than the prices paid and received by farmers, it is the generally accepted measure. The results show an approximately horizontal trend over the entire period. Furthermore, while the quality of farm products changed very little, the quality of manufactured goods was steadily improving (which is not reflected in that price index). The farmer, therefore, was in fact getting more for his money.

A more detailed study by Bowman and Keehn casts even more doubt on the hypothesis that the farmers were faced with unfavorable changes in relative prices.[1] They examined the terms of trade for four states—Illinois, Indiana, Iowa, and Wisconsin—where there was strong agricultural protest from 1870 to 1900. Twenty-two of the twenty-four indices of the terms of trade between agriculture and man-

Figure XI.2   AGRICULTURAL TERMS OF TRADE, 1865–1900[a]

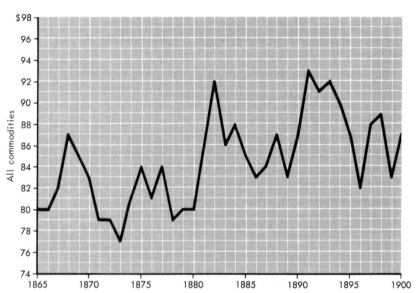

[a] These terms of trade are wholesale prices of farm products relative to prices of all commodities.

Source: *Hist. Statistics* (Washington: GPO, 1975), Part I, Ser. E 52–63, p. 202.

[1] John D. Bowman and Richard H. Keehn, "Agricultural Terms of Trade in Four Midwestern States, 1870–1900," *JEH*, XXXIV, No. 3 (September, 1974).

ufacturing show a relative improvement for the farmer. Perhaps most revealing is the increase in the income terms of trade (farm revenue divided by the price of nonagricultural goods) by an average of more than 3 percent annually for the four states. Bowman and Keehn concluded that there is no evidence of a generally worsening price or income position for Midwestern agriculture between 1880 and 1900.

Further evidence that farmers did not suffer during this period has been developed by Fogel and Rutner.[2] They concluded that from 1849 to 1899 there is no decade during which the average real income of farmers declined. In fact, the average annual rate of increase of real per capita farm income over this fifty-year period was 1.3 percent. Thus, there appears to be little empirical basis for the farmers' complaints that they were suffering economic hardship during the postbellum era. In terms of purchasing power and actual income, the farmer was doing reasonably well.

Second, consider the issue of railroad rates. Traditional evidence suggests that railroad rates fell more rapidly than other prices.[3] However, Robert Higgs has cast doubt on this proposition.[4] Higgs concluded that a proper index of prices received by farmers for the major crops (corn, cotton, and wheat) relative to railroad rates shows an approximately horizontal trend until the early 1890s. Between 1893 and 1896, the trend moves sharply against farmers. After 1896, there is real improvement in the farmers' position. However, an examination of the spread between the Liverpool price and the price on the farm shows that the divergence narrows strikingly over this entire period; the farmer was receiving a larger proportion of the total Liverpool sale price of a bushel of wheat. This is not surprising, considering how much ocean freight rates fell during this period. Since the ocean freight rate on wheat in 1900 was less than one-third the 1870 rate, clearly the farmers' percentage of the Liverpool price had improved dramatically.[5]

[2] Robert F. Fogel and Jack Rutner, "The Efficiency Effects of Federal Land Policy, 1850–1900: A Report of Some Provisional Findings," in William Aydelotte, et al., *The Dimensions of Quantitiative Research in History* (Princeton: Princeton University Press, 1972).

[3] For a summary description of decline in rail rates, see Fred S. Shannon, *The Farmers' Last Frontier* (New York: Holt, 1963), pp. 296–97.

[4] Robert Higgs, "Railroad Rates and the Populist Uprising," *Agricultural History*, XLIV, (July, 1970).

[5] Morton Rothstein, "America in the International Rivalry for the British Wheat Market, 1860–1914," *The Mississippi Valley Historical Review*, XLVII (December, 1960). For further statistical support, see Holbrook Working, "The Financial Results of Speculative Holding of Wheat," *Wheat Studies of the Food Research Institute*, VII (July, 1931), 405–38. On the narrowing of the difference in prices, see Henrietta Larson, "Wheat Farmer and Market in Minnesota, 1858–1900," *Studies in History, Economics, and Public Law* (New York: Columbia University, 1926), CXXII, 243–56; and J. Chester Bowen, *Wheat and Flour Prices from Farmer to Consumer*, U.S. Dept. of Labor, Bureau of Labor Statistics, Bulletin No. 130 (Washington, 1913), *passim.*

TABLE XI.1   Interest Rates and Capital Flows

Region	Mortgage Interest Rates, 1888	Movement of Funds, 1880–1920
New England	5.82	Outflow
Northeast	5.66	Outflow
South	7.91	Inflow
Middle West	7.10	Inflow
Great Plains	7.24	Inflow
Far West	10.43	Outflow

Source: Lance E. Davis, "The Investment Market, 1870–1914: The Evolution of a National Market," *JEH* (September, 1965).

Finally, let us look at the mortgage picture for farmers. It is surprising how few mortgaged farms there were in the United States during this time. Approximately 29 percent of the farms were mortgaged to 35 percent of their value. For the North Central area, where the complaints of the Populists were most vociferous, 38.7 percent of the farms were mortgaged in 1890. The states where most farms were mortgaged were Kansas with 60 percent and Nebraska with 54 percent.[6] Equally striking is the short life span of these mortgages. The average life of a farm mortgage in 1890 was 4.5 years for the North Central area, whereas those in Kansas and Nebraska were 3.6 and 3.7 years.[7] Since the mortgages were so short that there were no substantial changes in the price level over those brief periods of time, a falling price level with a fixed mortgage generally imposed no great hardship; and when farmers took out a new mortgage, they did so at a new rate. Only when periods of five years or more are considered did prices fall enough to cause some hardship.

The one place where there is some support for the farmers' position is in a regional comparison of mortgage interest rates. The average rate of interest was approximately 8.5 percent for Kansas and Nebraska, about 8 percent for the North Central area, and 5.5 percent for the Atlantic states. Although mortgage rates had fallen from 10 or 12 percent or more in the North Central area at an earlier date, it appears that imperfections in the capital market worked against the Western farmers in that they did not enjoy the same favorable rates of interest on mortgage loans as did Eastern farmers.[8] Or it may simply

[6] "Real Estate Mortgages," *Eleventh Census of the U.S., 1890*, p. 123 (Percentage of Farms Mortgaged).

[7] *Ibid.*, p. 109 (Life Span of Farm Mortgages).

[8] These come from *Eleventh Census of the U.S., 1890*, "Real Estate Mortgages," p. 259. Lance E. Davis makes a case for an imperfect capital market in "The Investment Market, 1870–1914: The Evolution of a National Market," *JEH*, XXV (September, 1965); however, it is hard to know how much of this was the increased risk of mortgages on the frontier compared with loans on farms in the East.

have been that sufficient time had not elapsed for capital markets to adjust to the interest rate differentials. Table XI.1 shows mortgage interest rates for six regions of the country in 1888. With the exception of the far West, where risk and gold discoveries may have contributed to the outflow, the direction of movements are consistent with capital markets' adjusting to the interest differentials.

These economic complaints do not appear to have been the fundamental causes of farm distress. It is true that many individual grievances were caused by monopoly power of the railroads, by middlemen, or by imperfections in the capital market. But had these situations been changed or modified anywhere along the line, the basic distress felt by the farmer would not have been alleviated.

THE SOURCES OF AGRARIAN UNREST

The causes of agrarian unrest lay deeper. What was fundamentally at stake in the farmers' discontent was, first of all, that they found themselves competing in a world market in which fluctuations in prices created great uncertainty. The bottom could drop out of their income because of a bumper crop at the other side of the world—in Argentina or Australia. When farmers suffered from a period of drought and poor crops, the higher prices they had learned to expect in such a case might not be forthcoming (if other areas had had a good crop year).

Let us examine in more detail what was happening to the agricultural sector during this period. First, the demand for major agricultural goods, particularly wheat, cotton, corn, and livestock, had been growing rapidly. In general, it is true that increasing demand for agricultural goods is based primarily on expanding population; therefore, as the United States' population grew, the demand for foodstuffs also grew rapidly. This domestic increase in demand was accompanied by a growing worldwide demand for agricultural goods, which the American economy was well situated to meet. Before the Civil War, the United States had been a major supplier of cotton and, sporadically, of wheat. But with the repeal of England's Corn Laws in the middle of the nineteenth century and with that nation's increasing industrialization, England became a major importer of wheat, and the United States became a major supplier of wheat for Britain and other European countries. Corn was used primarily to feed livestock; but livestock itself was in demand internationally, while cotton continued to be a leading American export. Thus, it is obvious that the international market formed an important component of the growing demand for American agriculture. On the supply side, as was already observed in the previous chapter, the westward movement opened up new land, and the development of transportation means encouraged settlers to move into these areas in response to high expected rates of return. Thus, the vast western half of America was settled.

This is not the whole story of the supply–demand relationship, however. Concurrent with the westward movement in America and the consequent rapid increase in the supply of agricultural products, particularly of wheat, other vast areas in the world were also becoming leading suppliers. Austrialia, Argentina, South Africa, the Ukraine of Russia, and even (for a while) India were all areas where a supply of wheat was evolving for the world market. In this competitive situation, nothing could prevent the price of agricultural commodities from fluctuating widely under varying conditions of climate and rainfall. A year of poor crops in the United States might coincide with bumper harvests in Australia, Argentina, and other parts of the world. As a result, the price of wheat would be depressed by the large quantity supplied, even though the share from western America was small. Similarly, it would be possible for the price to rise even with a bumper harvest in America if poor yields were obtained in other parts of the world. While the international market determined prices of wheat, cotton, and some other agricultural commodities, many other agricultural foodstuffs and raw materials were limited to the U.S. market. The vast domestic market was also subject to sharp variations in supply and price.

Agriculture labors under another difficulty. In the long run, it tends to produce only moderate returns, because of the ease of entry. High prices induced a rapid expansion of agricultue and an increase in supply as people moved to new lands. But the resultant expansion tended to decrease prices so that returns fell, until readjustment took place and marginal producers moved out of that sector into more profitable occupations. This point needs to be stressed: A competitive industry is one in which an adjustment is accomplished by producers' readily moving into the industry when expected returns are high and moving out of the industry when expected returns are low. Obviously, agriculture meets this definition. So it is far from surprising that in the last half of the nineteenth century, with surges of new farmers moving into the industry and a vast expansion of acreage under cultivation, lengthy periods of depressed prices resulted. During such periods, prices were so low that many farmers were unable to earn the normal rate of return.

In short, a vast process of worldwide adjustment was taking place in which the demand for agricultural commodities was growing rapidly, but the supply was growing in vast surges. Inevitably, there were times of high prices and above-normal returns countered by other times of very low prices and returns. When low yields resulted from poor rainfall or other natural conditions in an area, the outcome could be still more catastrophic, coupling a low yield to lower prices. Aggravating the difficulties caused by wide fluctuations in the prices of agricultural commodities was the fact that prices in general were falling. This worldwide price decline resulted from a market economy's self-adjustment to two current factors: On the one hand, aggregate output was expanding at a rapid pace; on the other hand, the money supply of the world, based on the amount of gold available, grew more slowly. More products competing for the same amount of money resulted in a steady fall in prices. Declining prices, as previously discussed, imposed an additional burden on debtor farmers who had not anticipated the decline.

As though these woes were not enough for nineteenth-century farmers, this was the era when they were becoming a minority in America. Throughout all of our earlier history, theirs had been a dominant voice in politics and in an essentially rural society. Now, they were being dispossessed by the growing industrial might of America and its rapid urbanization. The farmers keenly felt their deteriorating status. Their reading matter was full of warnings and complaints against the evils and moral decay of the city and its malign influence over the countryside. Their disenchantment was an inevitable component of the vast and complex socioeconomic phenomenon that was taking place, involving both the commercialization of agriculture on a vast scale in a worldwide market and the farmers' becoming increasingly a minority group in American society.

XII

Creation of an Industrial Giant and Problems of Monopoly, 1860–1914

Since the rise of industrial America was one of the major alterations in the economic structure of the nation, a more detailed examination of the move to large-scale manufacturing is in order. We can get a brief picture of this enormous expansion by looking at four cases that illustrate the combination of technological development with organizational ability responsible for this development.

TECHNOLOGY AND ORGANIZATION: FOUR INDUSTRIES

Steel certainly played a preeminent role. Iron had been the primary material used, along with wood, in machinery and in most durable goods. Then, in the 1850s, Henry Bessemer developed a process that revolutionized the manufacture of steel. Superior to wrought iron, having much greater tensile strength and hardness, steel rapidly replaced iron in many uses (most important, in rails) as its price came down with the development of the Bessemer process. But quality control was difficult in the Bessemer process, and each batch of steel tended to vary. The open-hearth process, developed in the 1860s, was slower and initially more expensive, but because it enabled far better quality control and could make use of scrap, it gradually replaced the Bessemer process. Both methods originally could use only a narrow range of iron ores, excluding any with substantial amounts of phosphorus. The development of a basic lining that absorbed these impurities was a later important development, first used in an open-hearth furnace in 1880.

Both the Bessemer and the open-hearth processes are most efficient when they are used in large-scale production; consequently, the new industry gradually developed large firms. In 1872, Andrew Carnegie launched Carnegie Steel Limited to manufacture steel rails. As time went on, he and his partners absorbed other firms and plants. In those days, the large amount of coal required to make steel (two tons for every ton of iron ore) led to the location of mills adjacent to coal fields. Carnegie combined organizational ability with access to the capital market and acquired or built successive plants to meet the expanding requirements of the steel industry. Other firms also developed. There was a rapid expansion of the steel industry as it rose from a mere 19,000 tons in 1867 to 10 million tons by 1900. As Andrew Carnegie is associated with the early developments of the steel industry, J.P. Morgan, financier, is associated with its giant consolidation and with the first billion-dollar corporation in the world. In 1901, Morgan pulled together all of Carnegie's properties, along with those of other major steel firms in the United States, to form the United States Steel Corporation.

The story of petroleum is somewhat different. There were no waiting markets for the sticky substance that oozed out of the ground in western Pennsylvania—it was regarded as a nuisance. Initially, interest was attracted to it for its possible use as an ingredient in patent medicine, and a number of Eastern interests sent a "Colonel" Drake out to see what could be done. It was Drake who conceived the idea of pumping the oil out of the ground. Once out and refined, the middleweight distillates such as kerosene became the main lighting source in America until they were replaced later by gas and electricity. The refineries built in the 1860s were small, costing little more than $400; but by 1880 a refinery cost $300,000, and by 1900, $1.3 million. As in the steel industry, the development of large-scale production and improvements in methods lowered the cost; the price of petroleum fell from 36 cents a gallon in 1863 to 8 cents a gallon in 1885.

Organization and development of the petroleum industry is inextricably associated with John D. Rockefeller. He consolidated the industry and initiated cheap transport methods, either by pressuring the railroads into developing them or by acquiring and developing pipelines for inexpensively carrying petroleum products to leading markets. Indeed, by the turn of the century the Standard Oil Company came to dominate the refining part of the industry completely, just as a new demand for petroleum products was appearing with the use of the internal combustion engine in the new automobile.

The electrical industry, unlike that of steel, had its theoretical problems solved rather early—many of them by Michael Faraday. The industry was waiting chiefly for the development of a satisfactory dynamo; and in this invention, Thomas Edison played a leading role. Edison, virtually synonymous with the electrical industry, was an unusual combination in American history: he was an inventor, an innovator, and often an entrepreneur. Like most entrepreneurs, however, even Edison made mistakes. A serious error was his persistence in using direct current even while other growing firms were stressing alternating current as a more advantageous means of distributing and using electricity. Nevertheless, Edison developed a host of uses for electricity, uses in which the electric light bulb and the entire system of electric lighting were critically important. The electricity industry became vital to manufacturing. The electric motor, especially designed for specific machines, made possible their more specialized and efficient use. Before Edison's time, an overhead belt (powered by a central source of steam or water power) had driven machines at a constant speed or at speeds varied by some system of reduction. An individual electric motor made it possible to turn off any machine or to operate each at a pace to match its particular function. Another development, the application of electricity to household appliances, continues even in the twentieth century as an industry of first-rate importance.

The automobile industry began at the end of the nineteenth century and has continued its major impact on the economy well into the twentieth century. For a long time, people had been experimenting with various devices for gaining locomotion by some automatic power. One of James Watt's partners experimented with a steam-powered automobile at a very early date; and in the 1860s and 1870s in France and Germany, numerous experiments were underway with various kinds of automobiles and with the internal combustion engine, which ultimately became the main source of power. There was a long period of experimentation and debate about what kind of engine and fuel would prove most efficient. Should it be electric or steam or internal combustion? Even after this question was settled, there remained— for the time being, anyway—a period of adjustment in designing a body style that once and for all would dissociate the automobile from the carriage-without-a-horse concept.

Henry Ford took well-established features of the internal combustion engine and combined them with a design that was definitely an automobile, not a horseless carriage. Then, using the ideas first developed by Eli Whitney regarding interchangeable parts and mass production, he formed an assembly line. The net result was a cheap, mass-produced Model T.

Each of these cases also illustrates another dramatic transformation that occurred in the American economy during the nineteenth century: the rise of the modern business enterprise with its numerous distinct operating units and dependence upon a salaried managerial class.[1] As the economy grew and as the individual firm undertook more of the stages of production, the monitoring and coordination of inputs came to depend more and more upon a hierarchical organization using hired managers. This change in the basic organizational framework had important implications for members of the economy, both at the entrepreneurial level and for the workers.

THE HEYDAY OF MONOPOLY

For the entrepreneur, a major task was bringing together enough capital to finance large-scale production. One of the most famous firms in this area was J.P. Morgan and Company, the famous investment banking firm that exercised enormous influence over the development of financial markets in America. Morgan himself, more than anyone else, was responsible for railroad consolidation in the latter part of the nineteenth century; he also organized a number of the more celebrated mergers and consolidations at this time, that resulting in the United States Steel Corporation being just one. If the investment banker performed the essential function of developing the long-term capital market and channeling the savings of Americans into industry, he also, by the end of the nineteenth century, posed a problem because of the growing consolidation of American business. This requires further examination.

As new industries developed in America and the pioneering firms earned large returns, these high returns attracted new firms into the industry. The resulting competition lowered prices and reduced the rates of return. It is not surprising that in the face of these reduced returns, businessmen attempted to collude. The entrepreneurs mentioned in the preceding brief illustrations were cited for their contributions to organization of the industry; some of them are equally celebrated for their role as ruthless promoters of collusive activities.

[1] See Alfred Chandler, Jr., *The Visible Hand* (Cambridge, Mass.: The Belknap Press, 1977). Chandler argues that prior to 1840 such business organizations were practically nonexistent.

Sometimes this collusion was nothing more than a pooling agreement that lasted only as long as the members kept a good eye on one another. Gradually, however, more sophisticated techniques were developed. In the 1880s, the trust became the typical form of enforcing agreements. The trust placed the control of a number of firms in the hands of a single board of directors; thus, no individual company could take advantage of price cutting to beat out its competitors, and all operated as a unit. The widespread creation of trusts cause such immense public reaction that in 1890 the Sherman Anti-Trust Act was passed, making trusts illegal and outlawing other monopolistic practices. It was many years later, however, before the Act became at all effective. The Northern Securities case of 1904, dissolving a famous railroad merger between E.H. Harriman and J.P. Morgan, and the even more spectacular dissolution of the Standard Oil Company in 1911 showed that the Sherman Act did have some teeth.[2]

The era around the turn of the century probably represented the high tide of mergers, and indeed of industrial concentration of major industries in the United States. Most observers believe that since that time, monopoly power—however defined—has not increased in America.

What accounted for the increase of mergers during that period? It is easy to explain why mergers were regarded favorably by business (for their part in eliminating competition and raising returns) and why they frequently were initiated by the investment banker who received a handsome reward for forming the consolidation; it is somewhat more difficult to explain the lack of even further industrial concentration in subsequent years. Some observers have put stress upon the Sherman Antitrust Act, subsequent acts such as the Clayton Act (passed in 1914), and more vigorous prosecutions by the Antitrust Division of the Department of Justice. Others have pointed to the success of new entrants into the field who have continuously overturned major firms; and the failure of large firms to hold their position in the economy in the face of competition from new firms suggests that this has, indeed, been important. Still others point to rapid technological change, which continually creates new, superior products to compete successfully with older ones. Whatever the causes, it does appear that the period at the turn of the century was the heyday for monopoly power—at least to the extent that industrial concentration promotes such power.

---

[2] A continuing problem for the courts was a good working definition of *monopoly*. Was it the percentage of the market that a firm controlled, the availability of close substitutes? Changing definition by the courts has led to changing policies.

THE WELFARE OF THE
WORKER IN THE ERA OF
THE ROBBER BARONS

With the advent of the large firm, it is often alleged that there was a dramatic concentration of wealth in the hands of a few with a concomitant exploitation of consumers and the working class. Trusts, monopolies, and cartels are seen as instruments through which those at the top of the economic structure lined their pockets at the expense of those at the bottom. Examples of collusion, rising industrial concentration, and conspicuous consumption are cited as evidence for this position.

In this era of aggressive industrial expansion, of the development of giant industries, and of entrepreneurs who have been labeled robber barons, what happened to the workers? Whether they were immigrants from the Old World or farm boys seeking their fortunes, the workers often found themselves in giant industrial firms and living in burgeoning cities filled with smoke, soot, filth—all conditions that, from our perspective, hardly appear favorable.

Working conditions in the big manufacturing firms and the social conditions of the sprawling new cities certainly left much to be desired. Yet we must note that the implicit, hypothetical alternative suggested by such a comparison is with today's society and with today's productive capacity. The relevant hypothetical alternative does not imply that the workers were exploited or that they experienced bad conditions in comparison with today's conditions. Rather, it examines the extent to which the robber baron deprived the worker at the time. The lurid history of aggressive entrepreneurs leaves little doubt that they frequently robbed one another. How badly they victimized the worker, however, depended on the effectiveness of monopolies. The correct hypothetical alternative, therefore, is to examine what would have happened to per capita income in the absence of monopoly profits.

For society as a whole, monopoly is objectionable because restraints on free entry into any industry result in a misallocation of resources, so that total output in the economy is reduced.[3] Directly applicable to the issue we are exploring here, however, is the assumption that monopoly profits were income that under competitive conditions would have gone to the rest of the population. By reassigning these profits to the rest of the population, we can see how much dif-

---

[3] There have been numerous attempts to measure the misallocation costs of monopoly. For example, see D.A. Worcester, Jr., "New Estimates of the Welfare Loss to Monopoly, United States: 1956–1969," *Southern Economic Journal*, V (October, 1973), p. 40. He finds the loss to be approximately 0.5 percent of national income.

ference they would have made to per capita income. From 1900 to 1909, corporate profits before taxes were 6.8 percent of the national income, which was approximately $20 billion. This would make corporate profits about $1.4 billion.[4] If we take the $1.4 billion as profit and substract from that the competitive rate of return on the nonfarm reproducible capital in America—that is, the rate that that capital would have earned had all the corporate enterprises been competitive—then the residual will be a crude estimate of the so-called excess profits of monopoly. We find that the nonfarm reproducible tangible assets are approximately $20 billion.[5] If we assume that 5 percent is a competitive rate of return, then $1 billion would be a competitive profit rate for all corporations. This leaves a monopoly residual of approximately $400 million. If we redistributed this amount among the total population in 1905, the addition to per capita income would be slightly less than $5. Average per capita income was about $250, so the addition would represent a 2 percent increase in per capita income.

Although these calculations suggest the income distribution effects of monopoly, a more important issue is whether or not the worker was becoming better off during this era. Fogel and Rutner have calculated the growth of the real wage in manufacturing from 1849 to 1899 at 1.1 percent annually.[6] A similar conclusion was reached by Albert Rees, who found that for the overlapping period from 1890 to 1914, real wages in manufacturing rose 39 percent.[7]

The general trend in per capita income also casts doubt on the hypothesis that a few were growing wealthy at the expense of others. The 2 percent annual increase in per capita income from the end of the Civil War to the beginning of World War I represents one of the longest periods of such growth in our history. It also appears that income distribution was reasonably constant during this period. Thus, to suggest that under a different set of circumstances consumers and workers would have done better is to hypothesize a rate of growth of per capita income and wages that has never existed in our country.

[4] There were probably some "monopoly profits" in unincorporated income, although not enough to influence significantly the figures used here.

[5] The actual figure for corporate reproducible tangible assets is $25 billion; however, we have allowed $5 billion for "watered" assets. This is certainly an overestimate of the extent to which this practice existed, but it serves to give an upward bias to the figure.

[6] Robert W. Fogel and Jack L. Rutner, "The Efficiency Effects of Federal Land Policy, 1850–1900."

[7] Albert Rees, *Real Wages in Manufacturing, 1890–1914* (Princeton, N.J.: Princeton University Press, 1961), p. 4.

A LESSON FROM HISTORY:

Is Inflation Necessary for Growth?

In the last several decades, efforts to control inflation have been largely unsuccessful. This is, in part, due to a general perception that reducing inflation is too costly because it lowers the rate of economic growth and raises unemployment. A widely accepted corollary is that inflation is a necessary evil in a growing economy; it is the price that we pay for growth and stability.

The lesson from history is quite different. There are many periods in the U.S. experience when growth occurred without any significant rise in the price level. During the years from 1867 to 1914, for example, prices fell an average of 1.3 percent a year so that prices were 45 percent lower in 1914 than they were in 1867. At the same time, real per capita incomes were increasing at approximately 2 percent a year, while the economy adjusted to rapid industrialization and increased commercialization of agriculture. The generally falling price level did not impede the adjustment process or the rate of economic growth.

In addition to inflation's being unnecessary for growth, it does not permanently lower the unemployment rate. There may be some very short-term reductions in unemployment during a period of unanticipated inflation, but once employees and employers learn what the rate of change, in prices really is, unemployment returns to its original level. Again, the record from the U.S. experience is clear. The rapid inflation of the 1970s did not result in any permanent lowering of the unemployment rate. For the years 1971–74, inflation was approximately 7 percent per year, and the unemployment rate averaged 5.5 percent. By the latter part of the decade, inflation reached almost 11 percent per year while the unemployment rate increased to 6.5 percent.

If inflation does not promote growth or full employment, what are the results of a generally decreasing value of money? Several negative impacts are obvious. First, since prices are a device for communicating information, inflation reduces the effectiveness of markets. With inflation, it is not clear whether rising prices signal changes in relative scarcity or whether they are simply part of the overall increase in the price level. Hence, neither producers nor consumers can be sure how to react. A second negative impact of inflation is "bracket creep." That is, as incomes rise with inflation, taxpayers are moved into higher tax brackets. Between 1960 and 1980 this caused the average working couple with two children to move from a 26 percent marginal tax rate to a 40 percent rate. As a result, a larger wedge has been driven between wages paid and wages taken home, and again the signals of the marketplace are hampered.

Two lessons follow from our historical experience with inflation. First, substantial increases in real per capita incomes have occurred without concomitant inflation. Second, inflation generates significant impediments (and few benefits) for the growth process. Therefore, there is little reason to believe that a higher growth rate can be purchased with rising prices.

Suggested reading:

Milton Friedman, "Nobel Lecture: Inflation and Unemployment," *Journal of Political Economy*, 85 (June, 1977).

XIII

The Destabilizing Nature of Growth

We have presented evidence that neither the sources of agrarian discontent nor the concern over industrial concentration can be attributed to falling real incomes. It appears that many of the economic reasons given by historians for the dissatisfaction of the late nineteenth century are not supported by data. Nevertheless, people did perceive themselves as being disadvantaged by economic events, and it is the perception that matters. How does one account for these changing perceptions about the legitimacy of the distribution of the gains from economic growth? One explanation is that there were frequent business cycles that were severe enough to cause a general dissatisfaction with the course the economy was taking. Although it is true that the 2 percent annual increase in real per capita income for the period does conceal significant variations in income, it is not clear that contractions were either more severe or more frequent than they had been earlier. Therefore, a more thorough explanation for the political and social unrest is necessary.

An important cause of social discontent can be found in the inherently destabilizing nature of economic growth. Growth seldom leaves the structure of the economy or the relative status of individuals intact. For instance, not all sectors grow at the same rate. During this period, manufacturing grew much more rapidly than agriculture. In 1859, 56 percent of the value added in commercial output was produced in agriculture, but by 1899 only 33 percent originated there. The numbers are almost reversed for manufacturing: 32 percent of value added came from manufacturing in 1859, and by 1899 that sector's share had risen to 53 percent.

To accomplish such a dramatic reversal in the relative importance of agriculture and manufacturing meant that resources had to be bid away from one sector for use in the other. For this to occur, it was necessary to have a more rapid increase in incomes in manufacturing than in agriculture. For instance, Fogel and Rutner have estimated that agricultural wage rates increased at less than half the rate of those in manufacturing from 1849 to 1899.[1] They also estimated that in order to equalize wages in 1899, agriculture would have to lose about one million workers. So, although people in agriculture were becoming better off in absolute terms, they did not perceive themselves as doing as well as other members of society. Their political influence was waning, and sons and daughters found it more difficult to remain on the farm.

As was discussed in Chapter XII, there is a second reason for the growing agrarian discontent during this time. Increasing demand for agricultural output usually means rents, or a return above the cost of production, for those already in agriculture. As more and more marginal land is brought into production, those who settled on superior land can often capture some pure profits. But because of the high productivity of the virgin land being settled during this period and because of the vast supply of that land, substantial rents were not generated. Therefore, agricultural output continually increased, but those who had been in farming for a long time reaped no particular benefits from the population and the income growth that caused the demand increases.

A major factor in the rapidly rising per capita income of this period was increased specialization. As people obeyed the law of comparative advantage and captured the gains from trade, substantial increases in productivity were generated. Such specialization occurred both in agriculture and in other sectors of the economy. The resulting income gains were not without costs, however, particularly in the form of increased interdependency in the economy. As farmers became more commercialized, price fluctuations had a much more severe effect on their income. Likewise, urban workers were almost entirely dependent on selling their labor in the marketplace and, hence, were also more vulnerable to changes in economic conditions.

---

[1] Robert F. Fogel and Jack Rutner, "The Efficiency Effects of Federal Land Policy, 1850–1900: A Report of Some Provisional Findings" in William Aydelotte, et al., *The Dimensions of Quantitative Research in History* (Princeton: Princeton University Press, 1972).

It is clear from the preceding discussion that entrepreneurs were very disruptive in the economy. They formed a creative, dynamic force that was capable of recognizing profit opportunities and exploiting them to the mutual advantage of themselves and other members of society. But they also affected the income and the status of those who did not perceive such profit opportunities or those who simply valued leisure more highly than did the entrepreneurs. As some individuals responded to the incentive structure by creating new products, by organizing different forms of production, and by bidding inputs away from previous uses, others found that they either had to respond or be left behind. Economic growth had obvious benefits: longer expected life, better health, and a greater opportunity to consume goods and services. But it also produced costs through changes in the community and family structures. The workplace became more impersonal while status and position became less predictable. As an indication of the change in the structure of the workplace, the average number of employees per firm in the five largest industries (ranked by value added) changed from 43 in 1860 to 127 in 1910.

Growth and specialization during this period also brought rapid urbanization. For instance, in 1850 only 15 percent of the population lived in cities of more than 2,500 people, whereas by 1910, 46 percent were residents of these urban areas. Consequently, there were increased problems with externalities. Throughout much of our history, there had been little reason to worry about property rights definition and enforcement of property rights for resources such as air and water. But they were becoming increasingly valuable. The incentive structure basically had been adequate in terms of internalizing benefits and costs of individual and group action, but it was now found to be lacking in several areas. In a very real sense, the government, which can use its coercive powers to define and enforce property rights, was not performing its function, and there was a need to restructure the institutions.

INSTITUTIONAL CHANGE, 1870–1914

There is ample evidence, then, that there was dissatisfaction with the country's basic institutions: changing relative status of individuals in the economy; increasing interdependency; creative but disruptive actions of entrepreneurs; spillover effects of an industrial, urban economy; and the reduction of personal exchanges throughout much of the society. We could predict from this that pressure would be generated for changing the rules of the game. And that is precisely what happened. From 1870 to 1914, there were institutional changes that altered the basic incentive structure of the society. Although the concerns that generated these pressures were real ones that grew out of a general dissatisfaction with some of the results of economic activity, the alterations in the basic institutional structure were not fortuitous. In an attempt to give the government the power to solve these pressing social problems, the constitutional barriers to large-scale rent seeking were effectively removed.

Most of the significant institutional changes made came through new interpretations of the Constitution—interpretations that dramatically redefined the role of government and made rent seeking much more likely to occur. The first major alteration came in 1877, when the Supreme Court heard *Munn* v. *Illinois,* a case that had its roots in agrarian unrest. In several midwestern states, legislatures had passed laws that attempted to regulate the rates of railroads and other businesses, such as grain storage facilities. Although many were confident that the Supreme Court would rule that such regulation was unconstitutional, that was not the case. The Court upheld the state laws and in the process formulated a new basis for government interference with economic activity. Chief Justice Morrison Waite wrote the majority opinion:

> Property does become clothed in the public interest when used in a public manner to make it a public consequence, and affect the community at large. When therefore, one devotes his property to a use in which the public has an interest, he, in effect grants to the public an interest in that use, and must submit to be controlled by the public for the common good, to the extent of the interest he has thus created.[2]

Previously the Supreme Court had upheld the power of the state to regulate economic activity under the doctrine of police power. However, its regulation had to be incidental to some other purpose. The idea that private property used in the public interest was subject to public regulation gave the government a broad new authority. Regulation in the public interest was such an ambiguous doctrine that both resource owners and nonowners found it in their interest to try to influence regulation. William C. Goudy, one of the lawyers involved in arguing *Munn* v. *Illinois,* captured well the thrust of the Supreme Court decision:

> If a majority of one legislature can fix prices for the minority, so in turn that minority can obtain power at another legislature and fix prices for the products or merchandise of their adversaries. When capital is in con-

[2] 94 U.S. 126 (1877).

trol the price will be fixed; when labor holds the power the investment of the capitalists must suffer. The price of corn may be made high today, and reduced tomorrow. All trade and commerce will be destroyed, and the struggle at the polls will be the natural substitute for natural laws of supply and demand.[3]

The ambiguity of the government's power to interfere with economic activities was furthered by the development of the doctrine of "reasonable regulation." During the 1870s and 1880s, there was considerable controversy about how the due process clauses of the Constitution should be interpreted. These controversies culminated in a case (*Chicago, Milwaukee and St. Paul Railroad Co.* v. *Minnesota*) in which the Supreme Court held that all state regulations must be reasonable. The definition of reasonableness, however, was left to lower courts to determine, with no constitutional provisions or principles of law for guidance. Therefore, it is not surprising that the definition of reasonableness changed over time, depending on the economic and social pressures of the moment. In 1898 the Supreme Court held that regulating the hours of miners was reasonable; but in 1905 it ruled that regulating the hours in bake shops was unreasonable. In the face of such an inconsistent doctrine, individuals found it increasingly worthwhile to devote resources to seeking favors from government or to prevent them from being taken away.

The encouragement of rent seeking was furthered by *McCray* v. *United States* in 1904. In this case, the Court upheld a statute that regulated margarine production by placing a tax of ten cents per pound on artificially colored margarine but only one-fourth of a cent per pound on the uncolored product. Prior to this, government had the power to tax, but it could not use it for such blatant nonrevenue purposes. Coupled with the Sixteenth Amendment, passed in 1913 (the income tax amendment), this case increased the potential for the state to be used by those who could capture it for their ends. It also meant that other individuals found it worthwhile to devote considerable resources to protecting their rights from takings through taxes.

Another important development was the "stream of commerce" doctrine, promulgated in *Swift and Co.* v. *United States* in 1905. In this case, the Court held that economic activities that might eventually be part of interstate commerce were subject to federal control. This doctrine has expanded until now almost all production and distribution is subject to such control because of its potential involvement in interstate commerce. Rather than providing a limit on state interference

---

[3] W.C. Goudy, *Munn and Scott, v. Illinois: Brief and Argument for Plaintiffs in Error*. Illinois Supreme Court (October Term, 1875).

with interstate trade, the commerce clause became a justification for federal interference and control.

Between 1892 and 1911, a series of cases helped to substantially expand the power of the legislative branch to grant discretionary power to the executive. Congress had only to outline the basic policy objectives, and a regulatory board or commission could then implement the mechanics of law, writing rules as it saw fit. In a 1911 ruling on *United States* v. *Grimaud*, the Court decreed that administrative rulings had the force of law. This executive lawmaking had serious implications for rent seeking. Special-interest "legislation" could now be obtained by convincing only the members of a small regulatory board of its merits.

As a response to the changing institutional environment, numerous mechanisms were developed for expanding the government's influence in the economy. The Interstate Commerce Commission, the first of many federal regulatory bodies, was created in 1887. The Federal Reserve System, created in 1914, allowed for a much more direct involvement of the federal government in manipulating the money supply. Although this allowed for more complete management of the nation's monetary system, it also created the hazard of inappropriate policy actions (see Chapter XIV).

As we have seen, during the latter part of the nineteenth century there was rapid economic growth. This growth was a response to a relatively efficient set of institutional constraints or basic rules that encouraged productivity and discouraged rent seeking. However, this growth also unleashed powerful forces that created strong pressures for institutional change. In the process of responding to these pressures, the rights structure that had provided the incentives for growth was altered.

XIV

War, Prosperity, Depression, and War, 1914–1945

The economic history of the twentieth century is very different from that of the nineteenth. The nineteenth century witnessed a growing international interdependence, an unequaled movement of people from Europe to newly settled lands, and a flow of capital to aid in their development. The spread of new scientific ideas and technology led to growth in many parts of the world. It is frequently argued that development during the nineteenth century was limited to a small part of the world; but compared with anything in the past, it was a century of unprecedented growth, one in which man could optimistically envision a continually advancing world. The twentieth century, on the other hand, has been dominated by two global wars and a severe depression—all leading to a fundamental reorientation of the economy, to a new role for government, and to a pessimistic view of the world's future—all of this despite the promise of modern technology.

TWENTIETH-CENTURY GROWTH

Before discussing the events of the twentieth century, it is useful to understand the pace and the pattern of growth during the period. Following the Civil War, the United States experienced relatively rapid economic growth. Immigrants in their prime working years flooded our shores and increased the amount of labor per capita. Westward expansion increased the availability of natural resources. At the same time, capital formation and technological change were making their contribution.

This expansion continued into the twentieth century, although at a slightly slower pace. The pre- and post–World War I years were prosperous ones with real net national product per capita growing at more than 2 percent per year. In terms of gross national product, the Roaring Twenties were not so roaring when compared with the first two decades (see Figure XIV.1). But even then, per capita incomes were growing at a rate that would cause them to double every forty years.

Figure XIV.1   TOTAL AND PER CAPITA GROSS NATIONAL PRODUCT, 1958 PRICES

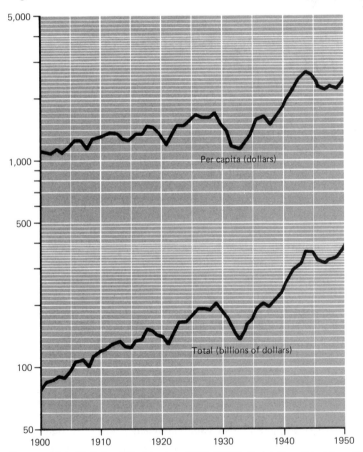

Source: *Hist. Statistics* (Washington: GPO, 1975), Part I, Ser. F 1–15, p. 224.

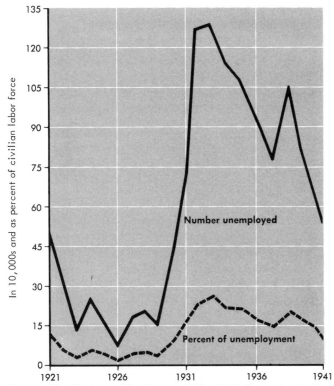

Source: *Hist. Statistics* (Washington: GPO, 1975), Part I, Ser. D 85–86, p. 135.

Figure XIV.2 UNEMPLOYMENT, 1921–1941

The Great Depression, of course, changed these trends. Between 1929 and 1937, real net national product per capita declined at a rate of 0.5 percent per year. Though there had been depressions in the past, this one was unprecedented in severity and length. The unemployment rates shown in Figure XIV.2 tell most of the story.

Following the Great Depression, the rate of growth in real per capita income accelerated to more than 3 percent per year. A word of caution is in order here about economic growth in a world at war. Our measures of economic growth capture changes in output and, therefore, are only a proxy for changes in welfare. During World War I and World War II much of our productive capacity was devoted to war materials. Though this may have contributed to our long-run well-being, it would be incorrect to infer that human welfare can be expanded by engaging in war. Efforts have been made to correct for this and similar problems with our measures of growth, and they show a level of well-being somewhat below the gross national product. By any measure, however, rates of growth during this period were significant.

THOSE ROARING TWENTIES

During war, resources are mobilized and diverted from the peacetime objective of satisfying consumers to the immediate objective of effectively implementing a war. It is not surprising, then, that when a war ends, the economy faces basic problems in dislocation as it returns to a consumer-oriented economy. A government must control and direct the flow of resources for implementing the war; and when the war ends, there is a tendency for government to maintain some of the controls. With the end of World War I in 1919, however, the United States seemed to be on its way back toward a consumer-oriented economy as rapid demobilization took place.

The first postwar cloud came with the sharp, brief recession of 1921. It has frequently been argued that this so-called "inventory recession" was caused by a rapid accumulation of inventories that could not be sold at existing prices. As a result, there was a sharp fall in prices and brief unemployment distress. Thereafter, however, the 1920s were a time of relative prosperity, with real disposable income per capita growing by 26 percent from 1922 to 1929.[1]

In the latter part of the decade, another distressing sign appeared: heavy speculation in the stock market. After 1927, and especially in 1929, investors became convinced that prosperity was here to stay and that they could make fortunes by buying and selling stock at a tremendous profit after it had been bid up by everyone else. It appeared that everyone entered the stock market with this in mind; and as they did, they continued to bid up prices. Many speculators bought on margin, borrowing funds, so that with very small amounts of their money they acquired large amounts of stock. This worked as long as the stocks kept rising: They could pay off the money they owed and still have substantial profits. But if the stock fell, investors could be in serious trouble. The stock market disaster in the fall of 1929 had an explosive character. There appeared to be no bottom. Stocks fell to such depths that they wiped out a tremendous number of investors, leaving them heavily indebted. Between 1929 and 1933, approximately four-fifths of the total value of stock disappeared. The fall was so precipitous that

---

[1] The decade was not equally prosperous for everyone. See Charles S. Holt, "Who Benefited from the Prosperity of the Twenties?" *EEH*, 14 (July, 1977), pp. 277–89.

it was not until the 1950s that stock prices recovered to their 1929 pre-crash level.

THE GREAT DEPRESSION EXAMINED

If the stock market triggered the Great Depression, it was certainly not the fundamental cause. The causes of depressions and cyclical instability are inherent in a free market economy. A market economy operates on the basis of the multiple decisions of consumers, savers, and investors. Producers play a key role here. They must make decisions in advance with respect to buying plant and equipment, buying raw materials, and employing workers, all before they receive any return. They are betting on what the demand will be for the goods they produce and, therefore, on what they will get in return. As risk takers, they are willing to invest when expectations look bright. Conversely, if the economic barometer seems to be falling, they will batten down the hatches and curtail investment; and with the fluctuation in investment, income fluctuates. If businesspeople do not invest, then income will fall. This tends to have cumulative effects. As less income becomes available, workers are laid off. When they are laid off and no longer able to buy more goods, the expectations of other businesspeople who are investing look dimmer, and they, too, curtail investments.

Understanding the cause of a depression, however, still requires an explanation of why the economic barometer is falling. Economists are certainly not in agreement on this issue, but most can be placed in one of two camps. The Keynesians, named after John Maynard Keynes, argue that the cause for the decline in the 1930s can be found in demand factors. Led most recently by Peter Temin, the Keynesians argue that external changes in consumption demand triggered a reduction in investment, which in turn sent the economy into its downward spiral.[2] The monetarists, on the other hand, believe that a moderate recession turned into a major depression because the Federal Reserve System allowed the money supply to decline by one-third between 1929 and 1933 (see Figure XIV.3). Milton Friedman and Anna Schwartz in *A Monetary History of the United States, 1867–1960*[3] ar-

---

[2] Peter Temin, *Did Monetary Forces Cause the Great Depression?* (New York: W.W. Norton and Company, Inc., 1976).

[3] Milton Friedman and Anna Schwartz, *A Monetary History of the United States, 1867–1960* (New York: National Bureau of Economic Research, 1963).

gued that it was this decline in the money supply that brought about reduced demand and investment.

The debate continues as both camps attempt to muster new theoretical explanations and evidence. Nevertheless, it is safe to say that consumption demand did decline and that getting the United States out of the Great Depression required an increase in that demand. Furthermore, there seems to be a growing consensus that an important relationship does exist between the money supply and demand. The failure of the Federal Reserve System to expand the money supply certainly aggravated the decline.

The magnitude of the Great Depression can be judged from Figures XIV.1 and XIV.2. A quarter of America's labor force was unemployed in 1932 and 1933, a level of unemployment unprecedented in

Figure XIV.3   MONEY SUPPLY,[a] **1925–1939**

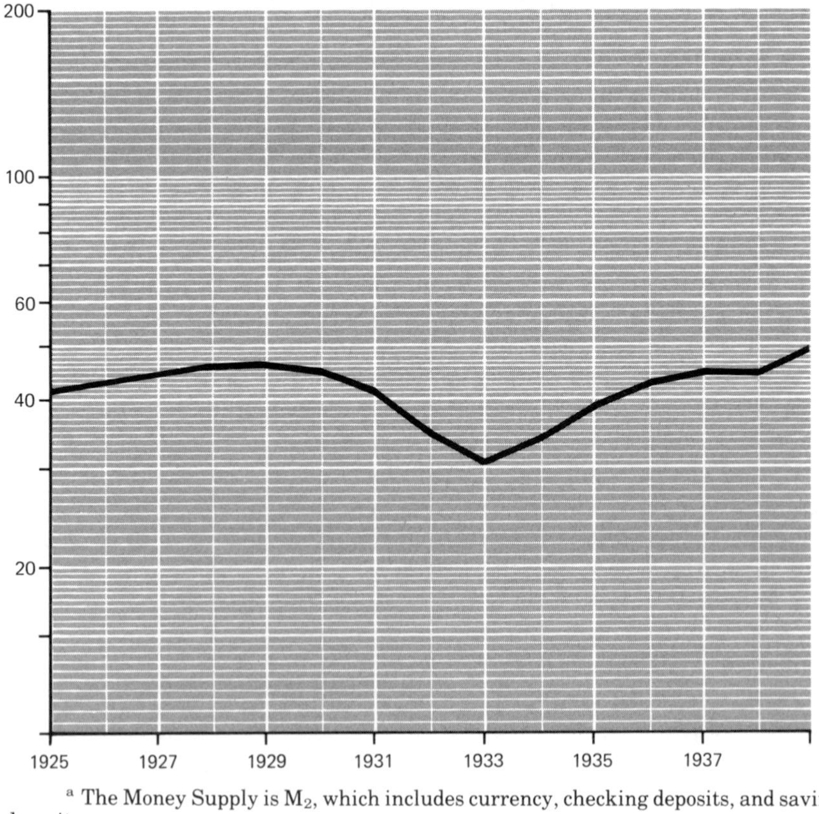

[a] The Money Supply is M_2, which includes currency, checking deposits, and saving deposits.

Source: Peter Temin, *Did Monetary Forces Cause the Great Depression?* (New York: W. W. Norton and Company, 1976), pp. 5–6.

American history. Moreover, they remained unemployed; and although there was gradual recovery, a substantial share of the labor force continued to be out of work during the the end of the decade.

THE NEW DEAL

In light of the anomalous character of the Great Depression, it is not surprising that the government should have been confused about how to cure it. The explanations just described also hold the key to potential cures for the Depression. On the Keynesian side, fiscal policy is seen as necessary for increasing aggregate demand. On the monetarist side, the cure is found in the supply of money. Unfortunately, it was not until we were well into the Depression that either fiscal or monetary policy moved in the direction of cure.

President Herbert Hoover made a first effort toward recovery by setting up the Reconstruction Finance Corporation (RFC) to make loans that would encourage business expansion despite bad times. With $1.5 billion available, the RFC was a step in the right direction, but the amount was too limited to block the swelling tide. A second effort was the Hawley–Smoot tariff act, which raised tariffs but provided only brief protection for some industries in import-competing goods at the expense of those engaged in exports. In order to help the farmer, Hoover set up the Farm Board to stabilize farm prices. But the $500 million appropriated for this purpose was soon exhausted, and prices continued to tumble.

When Franklin D. Roosevelt came into office in 1933 during the depths of the Depression, one of his first decisions was to close down the country's banking system. His first 100 days in office were marked by an unprecedented series of legislative acts designed to get the country back on its feet, and his success with the banking system was a move that inspired confidence in many people. Banks were audited, and those that appeared to be fundamentally sound were reopened with governmental encouragement and support.[4] His other legislation covered the whole gamut of activities of the New Deal, from setting up the Tennessee Valley Authority through the beginnings of social security legislation.

Roosevelt's first effort to get out of the Depression was aimed at raising prices. To encourage inflation, the gold standard was abandoned and gold was revalued. Next, the National Industrial Recovery

[4] After a four-day banking holiday, an emergency banking act was passed, giving the RFC authority to support sound banks; and when banks judged to be sound were reopened, the fears of depositors were allayed.

Act permitted industries to collude and organize cartels in order to raise prices and thereby give businesspeople an incentive to produce. The Agricultural Adjustment Act (the heir of the Farm Board) was designed to pay farmers to limit their production. It is easy now to see why these programs would not work. It is hard to imagine that prices could be substantially increased when there was such a tremendous unemployment of resources or that industry collusion would encourage consumer demand. Nevertheless, groping and courageous efforts were made to stimulate the desperately ailing economy.

Roosevelt then concentrated his efforts on what was called "priming the pump," or deficit financing. Obviously, deficit spending on its own would tend to encourage expansion, unless it led to curtailment of investment on the part of the private sector. The problem was that "priming the pump" was not enough. The amount of deficit spending was so small that it was unable to lift the economy out of the depths to which it had fallen.

While the fundamental objective of the Roosevelt administration was recovery, a secondary one was reform. As the Depression continued, people's faith in the market system as basically fair and reasonably efficient waned. It was replaced with an ideology that held that major government intervention was essential to a healthy and just society. Perhaps the most far-reaching legislation dealt with security for individuals. The security that once had depended on close family unity was gradually disappearing in the face of the impersonal characteristics of an evolving market economy. The aged and the sick could no longer depend on the family for support. It was argued that young people tended to underestimate what their needs would be in old age. A primary objective of a social security program, therefore, was to make provisions for old age security from the beginning of employment. With this objective in mind, Congress passed laws on old age and unemployment insurance and on workmen's compensation.

A second area of reform took place in securities and banking. The stock market crash as well as the failure of banks had convinced many that the underpinnings for both institutions were faulty. The Banking Act of 1933 divorced investment banking from commercial banking, and the Securities and Exchange Commission was established to regulate the stock market. The Federal Deposit Insurance Corporation was set up to insure all bank deposits up to $10,000 and a percentage of deposits over that amount, and the Banking Act of 1935 was passed to expand the authority of the Federal Reserve Bank in monetary affairs.

While the federal government expanded the powers and increased the number of regulatory agencies that were to improve the performance of business, the Norris–La Guardia Act was passed in 1932 to free trade unions from the threat of injunction. Unions were granted the right of collective bargaining first by section 7a of the National Industrial Recovery Act, and subsequently as that provision was restated in the National Labor Relations Act of 1935.

A final area of government intervention was public investment, the most noteworthy of which occurred in the area of water resources. The Tennessee Valley Authority was established to develop an integrated multipurpose complex of dams for navigation, flood control, power, and recreation. In the Northwest, the Grand Coulee Dam provided power, but its ultimate objective was to irrigate a million acres of the Columbia Basin. The underlying assumption was that the gains to society from such activities—that is, the social benefits—were greater than the private benefits and, therefore, were worthwhile, although not privately profitable ventures.

If the New Deal was so successful at increasing aggregate demand, why did it take this country so long to recover from the Depression? By 1940, almost 15 percent of the labor force—8 million people— still were out of work; and by 1941, 10 percent remained unemployed. The recovery of 1935 and 1936 was set back severely in 1937. Again, the policies of the Board of Governors of the Federal Reserve System frequently have been blamed, because they raised reserve requirements at the beginning of that year, thus reducing the money supply. As a result, the economy again fell back into depression and did not reemerge until 1939.

The second reason the New Deal met with only partial success has to do with the sharp increases in tax structure enacted at all levels of government during the 1930s. While it is true that total government purchases of goods and services expanded during this period, with the federal government leading the expansion, the tax yields necessary to maintain full employment more than kept pace. E. Cary Brown in his study of "Fiscal Policy in the Thirties: A Reappraisal" shows that when government deficits are compared with those necessary to maintain full employment, "estimates show that in 1929, a year of full employment, all governments combined had a deficit (federal surplus and state and local deficits), while 1933 to 1939, except for 1936, were years of surplus or years of approximate balance at full employment."[5]

What the New Deal failed to do, World War II did with vigor. Between 1941 and 1942, when we suddenly became involved in a global

[5] E. Cary Brown, "Fiscal Policy in the Thirties: A Reappraisal," *The Reinterpretation of American Economics History*, Robert Fogel and Stanley Engerman, eds. (New York: Harper and Row, 1971), p. 486.

war, we again became a full-employment economy. Government expenditures increased rapidly while the money supply expanded.

Though its policies did not achieve full employment and its implications for growth are at best equivocal, the New Deal might be judged a success if it had benefited the one-third of the nation who were "ill-clothed, ill-housed, and ill-fed," to use Roosevelt's famous phrase. Clearly, the New Deal anticipated such results from a number of its policies. For example, policies that were aimed at encouraging the growth of trade unions—such as the National Labor Relations Act and the Norris–LaGuardia Act—had the objective of expanding unionism in America; and it was commonly assumed that unions would thereby increase the income going to labor. Together with the rivalry that developed between the American Federation of Labor and the newly created Congress of Industrial Organizations, these acts did expand trade union membership from about 3 million in 1932 to 9 million in 1940. Similarly, the Fair Labor Standards Act established minimum wages for workers and was aimed at benefiting the lowest income groups. The price support program in agriculture, the subsidized low-cost housing for low income groups, and the social security program were all aimed in this direction. What were their results?

Figure XIV.4 shows disposable income of the top 1 percent and 5 percent of income groups between 1919 and 1946, and Figure XIV.5 shows the wealth of the top 1 percent of wealthholders in the United States. Both figures indicate that wealth and income became more unequally distributed in the 1920s and that after 1929 the percentage of wealth and income of the top holders declined. From 1933 to 1939, wealthholding was again more unequal, but the share of the top incomeholder continued to fall. The significant decline in inequality, however, came during the war years. It is equally evident that after the war, wealth and income again became somewhat more unequally distributed. During the 1930s there was a decline in the share of the highest income groups, but it appears to have gone to middle income groups. The lowest 20 percent of consumer units, in terms of their income, received 4.1 percent of total family personal income in 1935. They received 5 percent in 1947 and 4.6 percent in 1962.

In summary, it is not at all clear that New Deal measures provided any significant redistribution of income. The decline in the share of top wealth- and incomeholders came about as a result of the Depression, so there had been a significant decline by the time the New Deal began. The most significant decline is clearly related to the high progressive tax rates imposed during World War II. Moreover, the redistribution from the very rich seemed to favor middle-income rather than low-income groups.

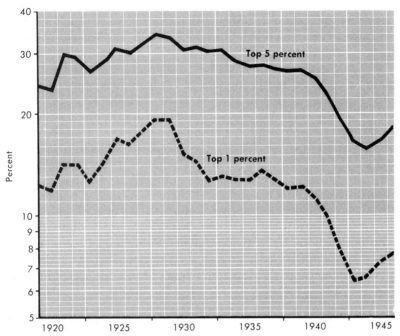

Source: *Hist. Statistics* (Washington: GPO, 1975), Part I, Ser. G 337–352, p. 302.

Figure XIV.4 PERCENT OF DISPOSABLE INCOME RECEIVED BY TOP INCOME GROUPS (TOTAL POPULATION, 1919–1949)

Figure XIV.5 SHARE OF PERSONAL-SECTOR WEALTH HELD BY TOP WEALTH-HOLDERS (SELECTED YEARS, 1922–1956)

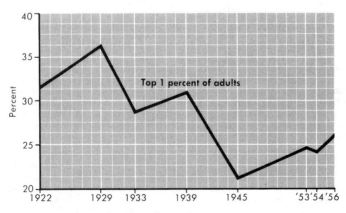

Source: Robert J. Lampman, *The Share of Top Wealth-Holders in National Wealth, 1922–1956*, A Study by the NBER (Princeton, N.J.: Princeton University Press, 1962), p. 25.

A careful examination of the measures designed to effect income redistribution suggests that the eventual overall result is not surprising. If incomes were redistributed in the 1930s, it was because the laws that were passed either facilitated a relative rise in the low-income group or transferred income from high-income to low-income groups. Minimum-wage laws and promotion of trade unions were aimed at facilitating a relative rise in the low-income group, but their effectiveness is debatable. It is not at all evident that minimum wage laws really raised wages of low-income groups. To the extent that they were effective and that the minimum wage exceeded that value of output of workers, the long-run result would be more unemployment and, therefore, more inequality in income. Similarly, even though trade unions may have raised the wages of their members, it is debatable whether they raised overall wages. Labor's share of national income appears to have been increasing, but this cannot be attributed solely to the unions.[6] Therefore, if trade unions had managed to raise their wages but did not influence labor's share of national income, then they did so at the expense of the three-quarters of the labor force that was unorganized.[7] Since this included most of the lowest wage earners, as a result incomes were made more unequal rather than more equal.

More effective results surely stem from differential tax rates and from the direct transfers of income from high to low income groups, as in the case of public housing and welfare. The magnitude of these transfers in the 1930s does not appear to have been significant, although the slight increase in the position of the lowest fifth of income earners in the 1940s suggests that the high progressive tax rates combined with welfare measures improved the status of the lowest income group during that decade. Furthermore, after adjusting for taxes, family size, transfers in kind, and education, Edgar Browning has shown that the percentage of income received by the lowest fifth of income earners rose by 45 percent between 1952 and 1972 while that received by the highest fifth of income earners declined by 11 percent.[8] These

[6] Labor's share of national income appears to have been increasing since about 1910, long before trade unions had any appreciable effect on the economy. A partial explanation is in the shift out of agriculture (self-employed entrepreneurial income) into wage status. For a more complete explanation, see Irving B. Kravis, "Relative Income Shares in Fact and Theory," *AER*, XLIX, No. 5 (December, 1959), 917–49.

[7] The impact of trade unions upon wages has been the subject of extensive inquiry. A study by H.G. Lewis, *Unionism and Relative Wages in the United States: An Empirical Enquiry* (Chicago: Chicago University, 1963), summarizes previous studies along with the author's own investigations. The result is an indispensable study for those who wish enlightenment on this controversial issue.

[8] Edgar K. Browning, "How Much Equality Can We Afford?" *The Public Interest*, 43 (Spring, 1976), p. 93.

results, however, were evident after the New Deal, suggesting that it was not even very effective in redistributing income.

HOW NEW WAS THE NEW DEAL?

The New Deal provided hope and encouragement to millions in a desperate era. It also elicited violent ephithets from businessmen and political conservatives. Viewed from a more detached perspective, what were the long-run consequences of the New Deal? What was its effect on the welfare of American society? Was the New Deal really a new deal?

We have already seen that the groundwork had been laid for the government to engage in rent-seeking activity (see Chapter XIII); this potential increased when President Woodrow Wilson asked for and received emergency executive powers to deal with World War I (the argument was that "extraordinary" conditions required "extraordinary" government intervention).

By 1917, the ability of government to intervene in the workings of the economy through fiscal policy had increased dramatically. The constraints on government intervention, the contract clause, the commerce clause, and the inviolability of private property rights had been replaced with new constitutional doctrines that could serve to legitimate almost any economic program. While the 1920s saw a reversion toward *laissez faire* doctrines, the Great Depression did provide the impetus for a greater governmental role in the economy. Constitutional precedent for this intervention was ample, though it required a divergence from the policies of the 1920s. The institutional environment that gave the government the authority to intervene in the economy was certainly not new. It had existed since the last quarter of the nineteenth century. But there was a new economic environment that generated the demand for government intervention. The combination of these two constituted the New Deal. Regulatory agencies added to the alphabet soup of agencies in Washington by establishing the TVA, the NLRB, the FDIC, the SEC, and so forth. Of the regulatory agencies in existence in 1966, fully half were created during the New Deal.

By the end of the 1930s, the role of government in the economy had changed. Government had become more involved as a result of efforts to get the economy out of its depression. There was also the assumption that the welfare of society could be improved if government intervened to reorganize and reallocate resources.

Perhaps the most fundamental change to come from the New Deal was the erosion of what has been termed the "fiscal constitution."[9] During every war and depression since the Revolutionary War, the federal government had run deficits. But in almost every case, these periods of deficit were followed by periods of budget surplus that were designed to reduce the debt. For example, between 1795 and 1812, surpluses reduced the debt incurred by the Revolutionary War by nearly one-half. When the War of 1812 increased the debt, surpluses from 1815 to 1836 reduced it by more than 70 percent. The $2.7 billion national debt that existed at the end of the Civil War was reduced to $961 million through twenty-eight consecutive years of budget surplus. The eleven years of surplus that followed World War I cut the government debt from $25.5 billion to $16.2 billion by 1930. Even in the years following the Great Depression and World War II there were some efforts to balance the budget. The seven years of surplus and seven years of deficit that occurred between 1947 and 1960 almost offset each other.

The Great Depression and Keynes's suggested policies for expansion served to erode that part of the unwritten constitution that required a balanced budget. No longer was there a fiscal constitution that limited the deficit spending of the government. In fact, the Full Employment Act of 1946 codified a new responsibility for government to maintain full employment, to stabilize prices, and to stimulate economic growth. As a result, deficit spending has become so commonplace that from 1960 to 1982 there was only one year, 1969, of budget surplus. In this sense, the New Deal was certainly new.

---

[9] James M. Buchanan and Richard E. Wagner, *Democracy in Deficit* (New York: Academic Press, 1977).

A LESSON FROM HISTORY:

How Did We Solve the Nineteenth-Century Wood Crisis?

There is growing concern today that resource shortages will constrain future economic growth. This concern exists because resources in heavy demand at any point in time appear critical to economic activity and because responses to growing scarcity lie in the future and therefore are difficult to foresee. Nevertheless, in the past, rising prices of scarce resources have encouraged technological change and substitutions so that resource scarcity has not provided an absolute limit to growth.

In both England and United States, wood was one of the more important raw materials in the nineteenth century, providing a major source of fuel, building material, and chemicals. As industrialization exhausted wood supplies, there was grave concern that the rising wood prices would limit continued economic expansion. However, in the face of rising scarcity, responses were many. Fossil fuels gradually replaced wood; and plywood, composed of what previously had been considered waste materials, became a common building material. Bridges, ships, and machinery, which were made of wood in 1800, were almost entirely constructed of iron or steel by 1900. All told, the response was immense. By 1954, per capita wood consumption in the United States had fallen to one-half of its 1900 level; most people had forgotten that a "wood crisis" had ever existed.

The lesson of substitution possibilities and technological change, however, is a difficult one to remember. The energy crisis of the 1970s again brought on predictions that the economy would collapse because of an increasing scarcity of fossil fuels. The desire to cushion the shock of rising energy prices and the failure to understand the importance of price alterations led to institutional changes that hampered the adaptive process. In particular, price controls on energy severely restricted the relevant information conveyed to both consumers and producers. Without this information, consumers could not know that energy was now scarcer and were not likely to seek appropriate substitutes. Producers were denied the opportunity to capture the full benefits from producing more or from providing substitution opportunities. Consequently, both demand and supply responses were impeded. Because we forgot the lesson from the wood crisis, the energy crisis continued for longer than necessary.

Suggested Reading:

Rosenberg, Nathan, "Innovative Responses to Material Shortages," *American Economic Review*, 63 (May, 1973).

XV

The Modern Dilemma: Government and the Economy

Our country's economy is fundamentally different today from the economy that existed in previous centuries. The basic mix of government and private activity has been altered significantly, the size of government has increased immensely, and the composition and level of government activities have been sharply transformed. This transformation reflects a basic dilemma of political economy: How can government be empowered to carry out its protective and productive roles without allowing individuals to use these powers for rent seeking?

GOVERNMENT'S EXPANDING ROLE

Since the beginning of World War II we have seen a rapid expansion of government expenditures (see Table XV.1). Although politically conservative opinion in the 1930s held that the Roosevelt Administration was spending us into bankruptcy, in retrospect growth of total government expenditures during the New Deal appears quite modest. From 1932 to 1940, federal, state, and local expenditures increased by 44 percent, while post–World War II decades recorded increases of more than 70 percent. When total expenditures are compared with the GNP, we see that there was an actual decline between 1932 and 1940. Since

TABLE XV.1 Real Federal, State, and Local Expenditures (1967 dollars), 1902–1980

	Billions of spending			Percentage of GNP		
Year	Total	Federal	State and Local	Total	Federal	State and Local
1902	6.1	1.9	4.2	7.3	2.2	5.1
1913	10.0	2.4	7.6	6.9	1.8	5.1
1922	17.8	6.5	11.3	11.4	4.4	7.0
1932	31.9	11.4	20.5	21.6	8.0	13.6
1940	45.9	19.1	26.8	20.3	9.1	11.2
1950	94.3	55.6	38.7	23.7	13.9	9.8
1960	172.6	103.9	68.7	30.4	18.3	12.1
1970	295.9	168.5	127.4	35.3	20.1	15.2
1980	369.2	232.1	137.1	36.5	22.9	13.6

Source: *Historical Statistics* (Washington: GPO, 1975), Part 1, Ser. E135–166, pp. 210–11; Part 1, Ser. F1–5, p. 224; Part 2, Ser Y457–465, pp. 1114–15; and Part 2, Ser. Y682–709, pp. 1127–28. *Economic Report of the President* (Washington: GPO, 1981), pp. 233 and 318.

1940, however, total government expenditures have gone from 20 percent of the GNP to more than 36 percent in 1980.

Changes in the distribution of government expenditures between 1902 and 1970 are shown in Table XV.2. Expenditures are classified by protective services (police and fire, and general control of financial administration, national defense and international relations, veterans', and interest); environmental services (highways, other transportation, sanitation, natural resources, parks and recreation); personal services (education, welfare, health and hospitals, housing and community redevelopment, farm subsidies); and trading services (post off-

TABLE XV.2 Abramovitz and Eliasberg's Four-Category Classification of Spending as a Percent of All Government Expenditures, 1902–1970

Year	Protective services	Environmental services	Personal services	Trading services
1902	43.6	19.2	23.6	13.6
1913	34.8	24.1	25.6	15.5
1922	40.9	23.2	25.3	10.5
1932	36.1	23.2	29.3	11.4
1940	27.9	27.7	32.5	8.2
1950	48.2	13.1	30.5	6.9
1960	51.9	13.8	27.4	6.9
1970	46.3	12.4	34.9	6.4

Source: Thomas E. Borcherding, ed. *Budgets and Bureaucrats: The Sources of Government Growth* (Durham, N.C. Duke University Press, 1977), p. 31.

ice and utilities). It appears that protective services have remained about the same during this period. Expenditures on environmental and trading services, on the other hand, have declined by 35 percent and 53 percent, respectively, with personal services expenditures rising by 48 percent.

We should be aware that these data represent only the expanding role of government as measured through expenditures. They say nothing about those private-sector activities that are a result of government's larger role. For example, it was estimated in 1979 that compliance with government regulations from safety to the environment required private-sector expenditures of $100 billion annually and that paperwork associated with regulation cost another $40 billion.[1] When lobbying efforts are also taken into account, it seems safe to conclude that government expenditures understate the actual expansion of government's role.

SOURCES AND CONSEQUENCES OF GOVERNMENT EXPANSION

The impetus for the growth in government expenditures during this century can be attributed to four categories of expenditures. The first is military expenditures, which expanded greatly because of our participation in two global wars and the tremendous costs of new military technology. Added to these have been the costs of the Cold War and the accompanying arms race. The second category is education. Expenditures here mirror the view (discussed in Chapter VIII) that the return to investment in human capital is higher for society than for the individual and that education should not be denied those who cannot pay. The result has been a spectacular growth in higher education with an unprecedented expansion in federal aid. Highway construction has also accounted for a large portion of increased expenditures. Between 1940 and 1979, the number of automobiles increased from 22 million to 105 million so that there is now more than one automobile for every two persons in the country. Trucks have progressively displaced railroads in hauling goods, and the growth in road and highway expenditures has been an inevitable consequence. Finally, public welfare expenditures have expanded dramatically. Ever since the New Deal there has been a persistent and growing conviction that poverty in the richest country in the world is an anomaly. This

---

[1] Murray Weidenbaum, "The Big Cost of Government Regulation," *Challenge*, November/December, 1979.

conviction has spawned a vast array of programs at the federal and state level. The farm price support program, the Office of Economic Opportunity, and state welfare programs all have one ostensible purpose in common: to redistribute income from the more affluent to the poor.

Some of the consequences of government expansion can be readily predicted by using our analysis in Chapter II. For example, the government purchases its military equipment from firms that specialize in producing such equipment. These firms have only one purchaser, and their survival depends on their ability to receive orders. It is not surprising, then, that they have intimate and powerful political ties with the federal bureaucrats and officeholders. The "military-industrial complex" is not an aberration, but the logical consequence of actions by organizations whose welfare or survival depends on federal government spending. Nor is it unique; it has its counterpart in every other voluntary organization that depends on government spending. Teacher organizations are among the more powerful state lobbies, although they are hardly more powerful than contractors and the construction unions that build highways. Welfare recipients have become a powerful political force, and environmental groups have entered the rent-seeking game. Between 1970 and 1980 the number of conservation organizations more than doubled. Membership in groups like the National Audubon Society, National Wildlife Federation, and Nature Conservancy increased more than 400 percent, and their annual budgets have reached as much as $30 million.

Despite the growth of government relative to the private sector, it is not clear that government has become more effective in solving the problems it attacks. It is no longer evident that the educational system is an unmitigated good or even that there is a very high rate of return on higher education. Not only are we less sure that we are producing the right amount of education, we do not even have a clear idea of what it is we are trying to produce. That is, we do not have a good measure of "output." We have built numerous highways on which we drive automobiles that cause most of the air pollution in America. Finally, despite spending billions of dollars annually ($234.7 billion in 1980) on transfer payments at the federal level, there is no conclusive evidence that the share of income going to the lowest income receivers has risen very much. What has gone wrong?

To answer this question, it is useful to compare consumer and producer decisions in the marketplace with those in the political arena. First, consider the consumer:

1.   Consumers who want to buy a product—a television set, for example—in the marketplace can directly purchase it. In contrast, if

they wish to buy more of a governmental service—say, crime protection—in the political system, they cannot buy it directly; they can only vote for the candidate they believe most likely to devote the desired fiscal resources to crime prevention. Whereas consumers in the market know they are going to get the television set, voters have only one vote and therefore do not know the outcome.

2.   This leads us to information costs. Information is never really free. It costs search time (which is time forgone from other activities) and sometimes requires direct money outlays for the purchase of informational material. Consumers buying a television have much more incentive to seek information about the desired product since they know that they are going to buy it. "Political purchasers," on the other hand, will remain rationally ignorant since the likelihood that their votes will make any difference is negligible. In fact, unless they believe that the prospective election may be close, they have little incentive to vote at all.

3.   Consumers buy a single product, but voters vote for a package of promises, since the office seekers run on a whole platform of issues. This raises still further the costs of information necessary to know what voters are voting for. Ideologies are substitutes for search costs. We buy a radical, liberal, conservative, or reactionary candidate rather than invest in the costs of really finding out about each issue.

Next turn to producers:

1.   A firm tries to maximize profits and competes with other firms by means of price, quality, and advertising. Office seekers try to put together and advertise the package of promises that will get them the greatest number of votes.

2.   A firm borrows funds from a financial institution on the promise of repayment with interest or a share of the profits. Office seekers receive campaign contributions from those who believe that they will further their interests. Individuals and groups with a big stake in the political outcome will be willing to invest heavily because the potential returns are great. For example, the organized crime element will find it worthwhile to invest heavily in candidates who (despite their campaign promises) will go easy on crime. Similar reasoning applies to public school teachers, firms subject to government regulation, and trade unions subject to governmental action. In general we are simply making the familiar point that government favors producer groups over consumers.

3.   To the firm, one consumer is like another. To the political representative this is not true. Voters often feel strongly about a single issue and will judge candidates on that issue alone. Hence a minority

of voters who feel strongly about an issue may be much more influential than the majority who are indifferent and will scatter their votes.

4. The most striking contrast of all is the measurement of performance. Governmental organizations nurture the growth of bureaucracy because the relationship between bureaucracy and the measurement of performance becomes more attenuated, the further decisions are removed from competitive conditions. In a competitive industry, a relatively inefficient bureaucracy would go bankrupt. However, no such constraint limits the growth of a nonmarket bureaucracy.

Although the preceeding characteristics of market and nonmarket decision making do not exhaust their differences, they do suggest why government may have become too large. Take education, for example. The "ideal" amount from the standpoint of efficiency would be where an additional dollar spent on education yielded a social rate of return just equal to that of a dollar spent elsewhere in the economy. This method assumes that we could measure educational output properly so that we could compare it with other investments. But even if such measurement techniques were available, there are interest groups—middle-income parents, teachers, and the students themselves—that receive concentrated benefits, or subsidies, that give them more clout than the general electorate who pays the costs of such activity. The result is likely to be "too much" education.

Another example of how these differences have led to rent seeking and increased size of government is the regulation of interstate commerce. The Interstate Commerce Commission (ICC) was established in 1887 to regulate the railroad industry in the public interest. It was easy to justify this regulation in light of some monopoly power held by railroads. But the railroads immediately found that they could accomplish with the ICC what they had failed to accomplish in the marketplace; that is, they now had an effective vehicle for forming cartels to set and enforce prices. Competition from trucking was met with regulation of interstate freight rates, which in turn reduced competition in trucking. The result has been higher transportation costs. For example, it was estimated that regulation caused interstate household moving rates to be between 26 and 67 percent higher than nonregulated rates in 1974.[2] Such regulation by the ICC has enabled holders of moving certificates allotted to a limited number of companies to obtain rents (rates of return above competitive rates). Thomas Moore estimates that rents for the top two revenue classes of all shippers

---

[2] Dennis A. Breen, "The Monopoly Value of Household-Goods Carrier Operating Certificates," *Journal of Law and Economics*, 20 (April, 1977), p. 53.

were between $2.1 billion and $3 billion in 1972.[3] Given the profits generated by restrictions on competition, it is not surprising that the trucking industry has spent considerable time and money opposing deregulation.

IS GROWTH OBSOLETE?

Although the preceding discussion suggests that certain areas of government have become too large, some would argue that a growing scarcity of resources in the world dictates an even larger role for government. Since prehistoric time, humans and their primitive weapons have brought destruction and sometimes extinction to many wild animals. As settlement replaced hunting, humans girdled the trees, destroyed the forests, and burned the land. When they huddled together in settlements, they produced air and water pollution. But these consequences of development and growth were not a major concern as long as there were endless forests and unlimited amounts of clean air and water.

By the end of the nineteenth century, however, these conditions no longer held in the United States. Industrial society brought with it noisome, polluted, nineteenth-century towns and cities with open sewers and coal smog. The cut-over forests of New England and the upper Midwest forced timber companies to move to the Pacific Northwest and the South as Gifford Pinchot and Theodore Roosevelt were expressing concern for the natural environment.

So what is new? There is really nothing new except the magnitude of the problem. More than 200 million people living in close proximity in an urban world continually affect one another so that externalities—or third-party effects—are a ubiquitous characteristic of our society. We have literally a mountain of waste material to dispose of each day. We demand power, but dams flood scarce wilderness areas; coal-fired generating plants pollute the air; nuclear plants heat water and emit potentially dangerous levels of radiation.

These conditions lead to a fitting question with which to end our study of U.S. economic history: Is growth obsolete? Modern-day Malthusians answer the question in the affirmative.[4] They argue that population growth and the accompanying consumption are running up against natural boundaries. With sophisticated computer analysis and

[3] Thomas Gale Moore, "Beneficiaries of Trucking Regulation," *Journal of Law and Economics*, 21 (October, 1978), p. 342.

[4] For an example, see Donella Meadows, Dennis L. Meadows, Jorgen Randers, and William W. Behrens, III, *The Limits to Growth* (New York: Universe Books, 1972).

TABLE XV.3 Indexes of Labor Plus Capital Inputs Per Unit of Extractive Output, 1870–1957

Year	All Extractive	Agriculture	Minerals	Forestry
1870–1900	134	132	210	59
1919	122	114	164	106
1957	60	61	47	90

Source: Harold J. Barnett and Chandler Morse, *Scarcity and Growth.* (Baltimore: Published for Resources for the Future, Inc., by The Johns Hopkins University Press, 1963), p. 8.

naïve models of consumption and resource constraints, neo-Malthusians are even predicting dates when the crisis will peak. In the world described by these models, the pie is no longer enlarging, and economic life is a zero-sum game. People subscribing to this position conclude that collective action is needed to constrain private action.

Perhaps the best example can be found in the "energy crisis" that was the result of OPEC restrictions on oil exports to the United States. As a result, the United States started down a collision path of growing demands and shrinking supplies of oil. Our collective solution to the problem of increasing scarcity was to restrict energy prices, to regulate producers and consumers, and to subsidize alternate energy production. A Department of Energy was added to the bureaucracy on October 1, 1977; by 1979 it spent nearly $8 billion and employed more than 21,000 individuals.

At this point, we must ask two important questions: First, is the energy crisis indicative of growing resource scarcity in general? Second, how does the collective solution to scarcity fit into the framework developed in Chapter II? The first question can be answered by noting that there is little evidence of growing resource scarcity. Harold Barnett and Chandler Morse measured scarcity between 1870 and 1957 by examining the labor and capital costs per unit of extractive products.[5] Their aggregate results suggest that rather than increasing scarcity, the period experienced decreasing scarcity (see Table XV.3). Agriculture and minerals show very dramatic declines in labor and capital costs per unit of output, while scarcity in the forest sector rose until 1919 and declined until 1957. Manuel Johnson, Frederick Bell, and James Bennett updated the Barnett and Morse data to 1970.[6] Their results indicate that the declining real costs of extractive output have

[5] Harold J. Barnett and Chandler Morse, *Scarcity and Growth* (Baltimore: Published for Resources for the Future, Inc., by The Johns Hopkins University Press, 1963).

[6] Manuel H. Johnson, Frederick W. Bell, and James T. Bennett, "Natural Resource Scarcity: Empirical Evidence and Public Policy," *Journal of Environmental Economics and Management*, VII (1980), pp. 256–71.

continued with no sign of an upturn. Hence, it does not appear that the "energy crisis" is indicative of any overall pattern of increasing resource scarcity.

Before turning to the second question, it is useful to consider the circumstances that have mitigated resource scarcity. Barnett and Morse have found that human responses to changing market prices have been the major force in reducing the pressure of such scarcity. First, price changes have induced people to seek substitutes. Examples of this abound in the area of fuels. Throughout our history, consumers have chosen among wood, bituminous coal, anthracite coal, manufactured gas, natural gas, fuel oil, and electricity. The rising price of oil in the 1970s induced people to find cheaper alternatives. Second, growing resource scarcity provides an incentive for technological change. The most dramatic example today can be found in the forest products industry, where everything from the logging operation to the use of "waste products" has gone through technological advances.

This leads to the second question of how our collective (government) approach to scarcity resource problems fits into the framework of Chapter II. Important to the mitigating circumstances just presented is the institutional framework that provided the incentives for people to respond. As long as the net private and social rates of return are equal, we can expect markets to cope well with resource allocation and to generate productivity. Clearly, the government has a protective role to ensure that private and social rates of return will be equal. In short, a market system operating through a structure of property rights provides signals that help resolve problems of scarcity. If property rights are altered so that these signals disappear or are distorted, shortages may not be resolved and, in fact, may become permanent.

When considering collective action, we must determine whether the signals regarding scarcity are correct and whether the institutions provide an incentive for people to react to the signals. Our efforts to regulate energy prices certainly have distorted the signals. By keeping prices low we have encouraged individuals to consume more energy rather than to seek substitutes. Furthermore, windfall-profit taxes and attenuation of property rights have discouraged private energy producers from exploring and finding cheaper substitutes. In this sense, the modern-day Malthusians who envision a dismal future may be right, but for the wrong reasons. Our future will not be dismal because resources are being used up but because the institutions are not providing proper signals and incentives for people to resolve the problems. Those times when people have succeeded in overcoming Malthusian cycles have occurred because they modified the institutional framework to promote productive activity. They have fallen prey to these cycles when the institutions have not provided the correct signals and incentives.

Hence, the modern dilemma of political economy is really that which has always faced us as a people: How can a government be given the coercive power to protect property rights and produce public goods without that power being used to encourage rent seeking? The economic history of the United States certainly provides some insights into this dilemma. We have sustained economic growth for more than 200 years through institutions that have provided the necessary incentives. Although that growth has lagged behind that of other developed nations in recent years, it is too early to make any predictions. We can say, however, that the future of growth will depend on our ability to resolve the modern dilemma.

Selected Bibliography

Chapter I

Cochran, Thomas C. "Economic History, Old and New," *American Historical Review*, LXXIV (June, 1969).

Easterlin, Richard A. "Why Isn't the Whole World Developed?" *Journal of Economic History*, XLI (March, 1981).

Fogel, Robert William. "The Specification Problem in Economic History," *Journal of Economic History*, XXVII (September, 1967).

Hartwell, R.M., and Robert Higgs. "Good Old Economic History," *American Historical Review*, LXXVI (April, 1971).

McCloskey, Donald. "Does the Past Have Useful Economics?" *Journal of Economic Literature*, XIV (June, 1976).

———. "The Achievements of the Cliometric School," *Journal of Economic History*, XXXVIII (March, 1978).

North, Douglass C. "Structure and Performance: The Task of Economic History," *Journal of Economic Literature*, 16 (September, 1978).

Rutten, Andrew. "But It Will Never Be Science, Either," *Journal of Economic History*, XL (March, 1980).

Chapter II

Buchanan, James. *The Limits of Liberty*. Chicago: University of Chicago Press, 1975.

———, Robert D. Tollison, and Gordon Tullock, eds. *Toward a Theory of the Rent-Seeking Society*. College Station: Texas A & M University Press, 1980.

Davis, Lance E. "It's a Long, Long Road to Tipperary, or Reflections on Organized Violence, Protection Rates, and Related Topics: The New Political History," *Journal of Economic History*, XL (March, 1980).

———, and Douglass C. North. *Institutional Change and American Economic Growth*. Cambridge, England: Cambridge University Press, 1971.

Field, Alexander James. "What is Wrong With Neoclassical Institutional Economics: A Critique with Special Reference to the North/Thomas Model of Pre-1500 Europe," *Explorations in Economic History*, 18 (April, 1981).

Hurst, James Willard. *Law and the Conditions of Freedom in the Nineteenth-Century United States.* Madison: University of Wisconsin Press, 1956.

Krueger, Anne O. "The Political Economy of the Rent-Seeking Society," *American Economic Review*, 65 (June, 1974).

McClelland, Peter D. "Cliometric Versus Institutional History," *Research in Economic History*, 3 (1978).

North, Douglass C. "A Framework for Analyzing the State in Economic History," *Explorations in Economic History*, 16 (July, 1979).

———. *Structure and Change in Economic History.* New York: Norton, 1981.

Tullock, Gordon. "The Cost of Transfers," *Kyklos*, 24 (1971).

Chapter III

Gallman, Robert E. "Commodity Output, 1839–1899," in National Bureau of Economic Research Conference on Research in Income and Wealth, *Trends in the American Economy in the Nineteenth Century.* New York: National Bureau of Economic Research, Inc., 1960.

———. "Gross National Product in the United States, 1834–1909," in National Bureau of Economic Research, Conference on Research in Income and Wealth, *Output, Employment, and Productivity in the United States after 1800.* New York: Columbia University Press, 1966.

———. "The Pace and Pattern of American Economic Growth," in Lance Davis, Richard Easterlin, William Parker, eds., *American Economic Growth.* New York: Harper and Row, 1972.

Higgs, Robert. *The Transformation of the American Economy, 1865–1914: An Essay in Interpretation.* New York: Wiley, 1971.

Kendrick, John W. *Productivity Trends in the United States.* Princeton: Princeton University Press, 1961.

Lebergott, Stanley. "Labor Force and Employment, 1800–1960," in National Bureau of Economic Research, Conference on Research in Income and Wealth, *Output, Employment, and Productivity in the United States after 1800.* New York: Columbia University Press, 1966.

Lee, Susan Previant, and Peter Passell. *A New Economic View of American History.* New York: Norton, 1979.

Lindert, Peter H., and Jeffrey G. Williamson. "Three Centuries of American Inequality," *Research in Economic History*, 1 (1976).

Ratner, Sidney, James H. Soltow, and Richard Sylla. *The Evolution of the American Economy.* New York: Basic Books, 1979.

Rosenberg, Nathan. *Technology and American Economic Growth.* New York: Harper and Row, 1972.

Chapter IV

Anderson, Terry L. "Economic Growth in Colonial New England: 'Statistical Renaissance,'" *Journal of Economic History*, XXXIX (March, 1979).

———. "Wealth Estimates for the New England Colonies, 1650–1709," *Explorations in Economic History*, 12 (April, 1975).

Ball, Duane E., and Gary M. Walton. "Agricultural Productivity Change in 18th-Century Pennsylvania," *Journal of Economic History*, XXXVI (March, 1976).

Bjork, Gordon C. "The Weaning of the American Economy: Independence,

Market Changes, and Economic Development," *Journal of Economic History*, XXIV (December, 1964).

Ekelund, Robert B., Jr., and Robert D. Tollison. *Mercantilism as a Rent-Seeking Society*. College Station: Texas A & M University Press, 1981.

Harper, Lawrence A. "The Effect of the Navigation Acts on the Thirteen Colonies," in R.B. Morris, ed. *The Era of the American Revolution*. New York: Columbia University Press, 1939.

Hughes, Jonathan R.T. *Social Control in the Colonial Economy*. Charlottesville: University Press of Virginia, 1976.

Jones, Alice Hanson. *Wealth of a Nation to Be: The American Colonies on the Eve of the Revolution*. New York: Columbia University Press, 1980.

McClelland, Peter D. "The Cost to America of British Imperial Policy," *American Economic Review*, LIX (May, 1969).

Morgan, Edmund S. *American Slavery–American Freedom: The Order of Colonial Virginia*. New York: Norton, 1975.

North, Douglass C., and Robert Paul Thomas. *The Rise of the Western World*. London: Cambridge University Press, 1973.

Perkins, Edwin J. *The Economy of Colonial America*. New York: Columbia University Press, 1980.

Shepherd, James, and Gary M. Walton. *Shipping, Maritime Trade, and the Economic Development of Colonial North America* (Cambridge, England: Cambridge University Press, 1972).

Thomas, Robert Paul. "A Quantitative Approach to the Study of the Effects of British Imperial Policy upon Colonial Welfare: Some Preliminary Findings," *Journal of Economic History*, XXV (December, 1965).

Walton, Gary M., and James F. Shepherd. *The Economic Rise of Early America*. Cambridge, England: Cambridge University Press, 1979.

Chapter V

Hamilton, Alexander, James Madison, and John Jay. *The Federalist Papers*. New York: New American Library, 1961.

Jaffa, Harry V. *How to Think About the American Revolution*. Durham, N.C.: Carolina Academic Press, 1978.

Johnson, E.A.J. *The Foundations of American Economic Freedom*. Minneapolis: University of Minnesota Press, 1973.

Kristol, Irving. "The American Revolution as a Successful Revolution," in *The American Revolution: Three Views*. New York: American Brands, 1975.

Shepherd, James, and Gary Walton. "Economic Change After the American Revolution: Pre- and Post-War Comparisons of Maritime Shipping and Trade," *Explorations in Economic History*, 13 (October, 1976).

Chapter VI

Abramovitz, Moses, and Paul David. "Reinterpreting Economic Growth: Parables and Realities," *American Economic Review, Papers and Proceedings*, 63 (May, 1973).

Adams, Donald R., Jr. "American Neutrality and Prosperity, 1793–1808: A Re-Consideration," *The Journal of Economic History*, XL (December, 1980).

Callahan, Colleen M., and William K. Hutchinson. "Antebellum Interregional Trade in Agricultural Goods: The Preliminary Results," *Journal of Economic History*, XL (March, 1980).

David, Paul.   "The Growth of Real Product in the United States Before 1840: New Evidence, Controlled Conjectures," *Journal of Economic History*, XXVII (June, 1967).

————.   *Technical Choice, Innovation and Economic Growth: Essays on American and British Experience in the Nineteenth Century.* Cambridge: Cambridge University Press, 1975.

Fogel, Robert William, and Stanley L. Engerman.   "A Model for the Explanation of Industrial Expansion during the Nineteenth Century: with an Application to the American Iron Industry," *Journal of Political Economy*, LXXVII (May/June, 1969).

Lindstrom, Diane.   "American Economic Growth Before 1840: New Evidence and New Directions," *Journal of Economic History*, XXXIX (March, 1979).

————.   *Economic Development in the Philadelphia Region, 1810–1850.* New York: Columbia University Press, 1978.

Mercer, Lloyd J.   "The Antebellum Interregional Trade Hypotheses: A Reexamination of Theory and Evidence," in Roger L. Ransom, Richard Sutch, and Gary M. Walton, eds., *Explorations in the New Economic History, Essays in Honor of Douglass C. North*, New York: Academic Press, 1982.

North, Douglass C.   *The Economic Growth of the United States, 1790–1860.* New York: Norton, 1966.

Paskoff, Paul F.   "Labor Productivity and Managerial Efficiency Against the Static Technology: The Pennsylvania Iron Industry, 1750–1800," *Journal of Economic History*, XL (March, 1980).

Pred, Allan R.   *Urban Growth and the Circulation of Information: The United States System of Cities, 1790–1840.* Cambridge, Mass.: Harvard University Press, 1973.

Rostow, W.W.   *The Stages of Economic Growth: A Non-Communist Manifesto.* Cambridge, England: Cambridge University Press, 1960.

Sylla, Richard.   "Forgotten Men of Money: Private Bankers in the Early U.S. History," *Journal of Economic History*, XXXVI (March, 1976).

Temin, Peter.   *The Jacksonian Economy.* New York: Norton, 1969.

Chapter VII

Andreano, Ralph L., ed.   *The Economic Impact of the American Civil War*, 2d ed. Cambridge, Mass.: Schenkman, 1967.

Conrad, Alfred H., and John R. Meyer.   "The Economics of Slavery in the Ante-Bellum South," *Journal of Political Economy*, LXVI (April, 1958).

David, Paul, Herbert Gutman, Richard Sutch, and Gavin Wright.   *Reckoning with Slavery.* Oxford, England: Oxford University Press, 1976.

————, and Peter Temin, "Slavery: The Progressive Institution?" *Journal of Economic History*, XXXIV (September, 1974).

Engerman, Stanley L., and Eugene D. Genovese.   *Race and Slavery in the Western Hemisphere: Quantitative Studies.* Princeton: Princeton University Press, 1975.

Fogel, Robert W., and Stanley L. Engerman.   *Time on the Cross.* Boston: Little, Brown, 1974.

Goldin, Claudia.   *Urban Slavery in the American South.* Chicago: University of Chicago Press, 1976.

————, and Frank Lewis. "The Economic Cost of the American Civil War: Estimates and Implications," *Journal of Economic History*, XXXV (June, 1975).

Gunderson, Gerald. "The Origins of the American Civil War," *Journal of Economic History*, XXXIV (December, 1974).

Higgs, Robert. *Competition and Coercion: Blacks in the American Economy, 1865–1914*. Cambridge, England: Cambridge University Press, 1977.

Parker, William N. "The South in the National Economy, 1865–1970," *Southern Economic Journal*, 46 (April, 1980).

Ransom, Roger, and Richard Sutch. *One Kind of Freedom: The Economic Consequences of Emancipation*. Cambridge, England: Cambridge University Press, 1977.

Reid, Joseph D., Jr. "Antebellum Southern Rental Contracts," *Explorations in Economic History*, 13 (January, 1976).

Wright, Gavin. *The Political Economy of the Cotton South*. New York: Norton, 1978.

Yasuba, Yasukichi. "The Profitability and Viability of Plantation Slavery in the United States," *Economic Studies Quarterly*, XII (September, 1961).

Chapter VIII

Davis, Lance E., and John Legler. "The Government in the American Economy, 1815–1902: A Quantitative Study," *Journal of Economic History*, XXVI (December, 1966).

Fishlow, Albert. "Levels of Nineteenth-Century Investment in Education," *Journal of Economic History*, XXVI (December, 1966).

Griliches, Zvi. "Research Costs and Social Returns: Hybrid Corn and Related Innovations," *Journal of Political Economy*, LXVI (October, 1958).

Hughes, Jonathan R.T. *The Governmental Habit: Economic Controls from Colonial Times to the Present*. New York: Basic Books, 1977.

MacAvoy, Paul W. *The Economic Effects of Regulation; The Trunk-Line Railroad Cartels and the Interstate Commerce Commission before 1900*. Cambridge, Mass.: M.I.T. Press, 1965.

Meeker, Edward. "The Improving Health of the U.S., 1850–1915," *Explorations in Economic History*, 10 (Summer, 1972).

————. "The Social Rate of Return on Investment in Public Health, 1880–1910," *Journal of Economic History*, XXXIV (June, 1974).

Ruttan, Vernon W. "Bureaucratic Productivity: The Case of Agricultural Research," *Public Choice*, 35 (1980).

Scheiber, Harry N. "Property Law, Expropriation, and Resource Allocation by Government: United States, 1789–1910," *Journal of Economic History*, XXXIII (March, 1973).

Chapter IX

Fishlow, Albert. *Railroads and the Transformation of the Ante-Bellum Economy*. Cambridge, Mass.: Harvard University Press, 1965.

Fogel, Robert William. *Railroads and American Economic Growth: Essays in Econometric History*. Baltimore: Johns Hopkins Press, 1964.

————. "Notes on the Social Savings Controversy," *Journal of Economic History*, XXXIX (March, 1979).

Goodrich, Carter, and others. *Canals and American Economic Growth*. New York: Columbia University Press, 1960.

Haites, Eric F., James Mak, and Gary M. Walton. *Western River Transportation: The Era of Early Development, 1810–1890.* Baltimore: Johns Hopkins University Press, 1975.

Mercer, Lloyd J. "Building Ahead of Demand: Some Evidence for the Land Grant Railroads," *Journal of Economic History*, XXXIV (June, 1974).

North, Douglass C. "Ocean Freight Rates and Economic Development, 1750–1913," *Journal of Economic History*, XVIII (December, 1958).

———. "The Role of Transportation in the Economic Development of North America," in *Les grandes voies dans le monde, XVᵉ–XIXᵉ siècles* (Paris: SEVPEN, 1965).

———. "Sources of Productivity Change in Ocean Shipping, 1600–1850," *Journal of Political Economy*, LXXVI (September/October, 1968).

Ransom, Roger L. "Interregional Canals and Economic Specialization in the Antebellum United States," *Explorations in Entrepreneurial History*, V (Fall, 1967).

Chapter X

Anderson, Terry L., and Peter J. Hill. "The Evolution of Property Rights: A Study of the American West," *Journal of Law and Economics*, 18 (April, 1975).

Bogue, Allan G., and Margaret B. Bogue. "'Profits' and the Frontier Land Speculator," *Journal of Economic History*, XVII (March, 1957).

Dennen, R. Taylor. "Cattlemen's Associations and Property Rights in Land in the American West," *Explorations in Economic History*, 13 (October, 1976).

———. "Some Efficiency Effects of 19th-Century Land Policy: A Dynamic Analysis," *Agricultural History*, 15 (October, 1977).

Fogel, Robert William, and Jack Rutner. "The Efficiency Effects of Federal Land Policy, 1850–1900: A Report of Some Provisional Findings," in William Aydelotte and others, eds., *Dimensions of Quantitative Research in History.* Princeton: Princeton University Press, 1972.

Johnson, Ronald N., and Gary D. Libecap. "Agency Costs and the Assignment of Property Rights: The Case of Southwestern Indian Reservations," *Southern Economic Journal*, 47 (October, 1980).

Libecap, Gary D. *Locking Up the Range.* Cambridge, Mass.: Ballinger Publishing Co. and the Pacific Institute, 1981.

———, and Ronald N. Johnson. "Property Rights, 19th Century Federal Timber Policy, and the Conservation Movement," *Journal of Economic History*, XXXIX (March, 1979).

Swierenga, Robert P. "The Equity Effect of Public Land Speculation in Iowa: Large Versus Small Speculators," *Journal of Economic History*, XXXIV (December, 1974).

———. *Pioneers and Profits: Land Speculation of the Iowa Frontier.* Ames: Iowa State University Press, 1968.

Chapter XI

Bogue, Allan G. *Money at Interest: The Farm Mortgage on the Middle Border.* Ithaca: Cornell University Press, 1955.

Bowman, John, and Richard Keehn. "Agricultural Terms of Trade in Four Midwestern States, 1870–1900," *Journal of Economic History*, XXXIV (September, 1974).

Easterlin, Richard.   "Population Change and Farm Settlement in the Northern U.S.," *Journal of Economic History*, XXXVI (March, 1976).

Fraundorf, Martha Norby.   "Relative Earnings of Native and Foreign-Born Women," *Explorations in Economic History*, 15 (April, 1978).

Higgs, Robert.   "Railroad Rates and the Populist Uprising," *Agricultural History*, XLIV (July, 1970).

———.   "Patterns of Farm Rental in the Georgia Cotton Belt, 1880–1900," *Journal of Economic History*, XXXIV (June, 1974).

Hill, Peter, J.   "Relative Skill and Income Levels of Native and Foreign Born Workers in the United States," *Explorations in Economic History*, 12 (January, 1975).

James, John A.   *Money and Capital Markets in Postbellum America*. Princeton: Princeton University Press, 1978.

Lewis, Frank D.   "Explaining the Shift of Labor From Agriculture to Industry in the United States: 1869–1899," *Journal of Economic History*, XXXIX (September, 1979).

Lurie, Jonathan.   "Speculation, Risk, and Profits: The Ambivalent Agrarian in the Late Nineteenth Century," *Agricultural History*, XLVI (April, 1972).

Mayhew, Anne.   "A Reappraisal of the Causes of Farm Protest in the United States, 1870–1900," *Journal of Economic History*, XXXII (June, 1972).

McGuire, Robert A.   "Economic Causes of Late Nineteenth-Century Agrarian Unrest," *Journal of Economic History*, XLI (December, 1981).

Parker, William N.   "Sources of Agricultural Productivity in the Nineteenth Century," *Journal of Farm Economics*, IL (December, 1967).

Riefler, Roger F.   "Nineteenth-Century Urbanization Patterns in the United States," *Journal of Economic History*, XXXIX (December, 1979).

Shergold, Peter R.   "Relative Skill and Income Levels of Native- and Foreign-Born Workers: A Re-examination," *Explorations in Economic History*, 13 (October, 1976).

Smiley, Gene.   "Interest Rate Movement in the United States, 1888–1930," *The Journal of Economic History*, 35 (September, 1975).

———.   "Regional Variation in Bank Loan Rates in the Interwar Years," *Journal of Economic History*, XLI (December, 1981).

Vedder, Richard K., and Lowell E. Gallaway.   "Population Transfers and the Postbellum Adjustment to Economic Dislocation, 1870–1920," *Journal of Economic History*, XL (March, 1980).

Williamson, Jeffrey G.   *Late Nineteenth Century American Development*. Cambridge: Cambridge University Press, 1975.

Chapter XII

Chandler, Alfred D.   *The Visible Hand: The Managerial Revolution in American Business*. Cambridge, Mass.: Harvard University Press, 1977.

Cochran, Thomas C.   *200 Years of American Business*. New York: Basic Books, 1977.

Higgs, Robert.   "American Inventiveness, 1870–1920," *Journal of Political Economy*, LXXIX (May/June, 1971).

———.   "Cities and Yankee Ingenuity, 1870–1920" in Kenneth T. Jackson and Stanley Schultz, eds., *Cities in American History*. New York: Knopf, 1972.

McGee, John S.   "Predatory Price Cutting: The Standard Oil (N.J.) Case," *Journal of Law and Economics*, I (1958).

Rees, Albert.   *Real Wages in Manufacturing, 1890–1914*. Princeton: Princeton University Press, 1961.

Schmookler, Jacob.   *Invention and Economic Growth*. Cambridge, Mass.: Harvard University Press, 1966.

Temin, Peter.   *Iron and Steel in Nineteenth-Century America: An Economic Inquiry*. Cambridge, Mass.: M.I.T. Press, 1964.

Weiss, Thomas.   "Economies of Scale in 19th Century Economic Growth," *Journal of Economic History*, XXXVI (March, 1976).

Chapter XIII

Anderson, Terry L., and Peter J. Hill.   *The Birth of a Transfer Society*. Stanford, Cal.: Hoover Institution Press, 1980.

Edwards, Richard.   *Contested Terrain: The Transformation of the Work Place in the Twentieth Century*. New York: Basic Books, 1979.

Gutman, Herbert C.   *Work, Culture, and Society in Industrializing America*. New York: Knopf, 1976.

Kelly, Alfred H., and Winfred A. Harbison.   *The American Constitution*. New York: Norton, 1976.

McCurdy, Charles W.   "American Law and the Marketing Structure of the Large Corporation, 1875–1890," *Journal of Economic History*, XXXVIII (September, 1978).

Mulligan, William H., Jr.   "Mechanization and Work in the American Shoe Industry: Lynn, Massachusetts, 1852–1883," *Journal of Economic History*, XLI (March, 1981).

Ransom, Roger L.   *Coping with Capitalism: The Economic Transformation of the United States, 1776–1980*, Englewood Cliffs, N.J.: Prentice-Hall, 1981.

Rosenberg, Nathan.   "Factors Affecting the Diffusion of Technology," *Explorations in Economic History*, 10 (Fall, 1972).

Scheiber, Harry N.   "Regulations, Property Rights, and Definition of 'The Market': Law and the American Economy," *Journal of Economic History*, XLI (March, 1981).

Chapter XIV

Benjamin, Daniel K., and Lewis A. Kochin.   "Searching for an Explanation of Unemployment in Interwar Britain," *Journal of Political Economy*, 3 (June, 1979).

Brown, E. Cary.   "Fiscal Policy in the 'Thirties: A Reappraisal," *American Economic Review*, XLVI (December, 1956).

Brunner, Karl, ed.   *The Great Depression Revisited*. Boston: Martinus Nijhoff Publishing, 1981.

Buchanan, James M., and Richard E. Wagner.   *Democracy in Deficit: The Political Legacy of Lord Keynes*. New York: Academic Press, 1977.

Friedman, Milton, and Anna J. Schwartz.   *A Monetary History of the United States, 1867–1960*. Princeton: Princeton University Press, 1963.

Holt, Charles F.   "Who Benefited from the Prosperity of the Twenties?" *Explorations in Economic History*, 14 (July, 1977).

Kuznets, Simon, assisted by Elizabeth Jenks.   *Shares of Upper Income Groups in Income and Saving.* New York: National Bureau of Economic Research, 1953.

Lampman, Robert J.   *The Share of Top Wealth-Holders in National Wealth, 1922–1956.* Princeton: Princeton University Press, 1962.

Mayer, Thomas.   "Money and the Great Depression: A Critique of Professor Temin's Thesis," *Explorations in Economic History,* 15 (April, 1978).

Meltzer, Allen.   "Money and Other Explanations of the Start of the Great Depression," *Journal of Monetary Economics,* 2 (October, 1976).

Temin, Peter.   *Did Monetary Forces Cause the Great Depression?* New York: Norton, 1976.

Wagner, Richard E., and Robert D. Tollison.   *Balanced Budgets, Fiscal Responsibility, and the Constitution.* San Francisco: Cato Institute, 1980.

Wallis, John Joseph, and Daniel K. Benjamin.   "Public Relief and Private Employment in the Great Depression," *Journal of Economic History,* XLI (March, 1981).

Walton, Gary M., ed.   *Regulatory Change in an Atmosphere of Crisis: Current Implications of the Roosevelt Years.* New York: Academic Press, 1979.

Wicker, Elmus.   "A Reconsideration of the Causes of the Banking Panic of 1930," *Journal of Economic History,* XL (September, 1980).

Chapter XV

Barnett, Harold J., and Chandler Morse.   *Scarcity and Growth: The Economics of Natural Resource Availability.* Baltimore: Johns Hopkins Press, 1963.

Borcherding, Thomas E., ed.   *Budgets and Bureaucrats: The Sources of Government Growth.* Durham, N.C.: Duke University Press, 1977.

Meadows, Donella H., et al.   *The Limits to Growth.* New York: Universe Books, 1972.

Meltzer, Allan H., and Scott F. Richard.   "Why Government Grows (and Grows) in a Democracy," *The Public Interest,* 52 (Summer, 1978).

Ransom, Roger L.   "In Search of Security: The Growth of Government Spending in the United States, 1902–1970," in Roger L. Ransom, Richard Sutch, and Gary M. Walton, eds., *Explorations in the New Economic History, Essays in Honor of Douglass C. North.* New York: Academic Press, 1982.

Simon, Julian L.   *The Ultimate Resource.* Princeton: Princeton University Press, 1981.

Smith, V. Kerry.   "The Ames–Rosenberg Hypothesis and the Role of Natural Resources in the Production of Technology," *Explorations in Economic History,* 15 (July, 1978).

———, ed.   *Scarcity and Growth Reconsidered.* Baltimore: Johns Hopkins University Press, 1979.

Index